A Call to Dissent

A Call to Dissent

Defending Democracy against Extremism and Populism

STUART SIM

EDINBURGH
University Press

Edinburgh University Press is one of the leading university presses in the UK. We publish academic books and journals in our selected subject areas across the humanities and social sciences, combining cutting-edge scholarship with high editorial and production values to produce academic works of lasting importance. For more information visit our website: edinburghuniversitypress.com

Edinburgh University Press Ltd
The Tun – Holyrood Road
12(2f) Jackson's Entry
Edinburgh EH8 8PJ

Typeset in 11/13 Adobe Garamond
by Manila Typesetting Company, and
printed and bound in Great Britain

A CIP record for this book is available from the British Library

ISBN 978 1 4744 9494 6 (hardback)
ISBN 978 1 4744 9495 3 (paperback)
ISBN 978 1 4744 9496 0 (webready PDF)
ISBN 978 1 4744 9497 7 (epub)

Contents

Acknowledgements

My thanks go to everyone at Edinburgh University Press for helping to get this project off the ground, particularly Jen Daly, Gillian Leslie, Ersev Ersoy and the rest of the Politics team. Also to the readers of the proposal and then the manuscript for their astute suggestions for amendments and additions to the book's themes, and to Prof. W. R. Owens for passing on some useful references. The support and encouragement of my wife, Dr Helene Brandon, has, as ever, proved to be a vital element in seeing this through to conclusion.

Introduction: Addressing the Politics of Dissent

Do you consider yourself to be 'woke'? When the term first emerged it meant to be socially conscious, an attitude you would assume anyone of a liberal disposition would naturally aspire towards. It meant you were in favour of equal rights and against discrimination in general: what could possibly be objectionable about that? Yet the political right saw things very differently indeed. 'Woke' has come to be used by people on the right more and more as an insult, a way to dismiss the validity of viewpoints other than their own. To be woke was to be 'not one of us' and it meant that your opinions and beliefs were just plain wrong, or even dangerous to society. As far as the right was concerned, such views were to be suppressed for the greater good. There was enough support for this position to merit the founding in the UK in 2021 of a TV channel dedicated to attacking the woke outlook: GB News. Although the channel denies it, there are distinct similarities to be noted between GB News and Fox News in America. The latter has become infamous for its biased reporting on the US political scene and the Trump presidency in particular. Whether GB News proves to be as successful as Fox News has been is hard to say at this stage. What is clear, however, is that there is a substantial audience for anti-woke sentiment. As long as that exists there will be openings for such ventures.

The campaign against woke is just the latest instalment of a general turn against dissent in Western culture. This is a consequence of what Wendy Brown has described as an unmistakable 'rise in antidemocratic politics' there that still blights our lives.[1] In its wake dogmatism, prejudice and bigotry are becoming ever more evident features in our social interactions. This development has had a distinctly negative impact on public life. Globally, authoritarian governments are striving to close down critical voices in both their political opponents and the mainstream media. If we are to counteract the dramatic rise of a reactionary right-wing populism, then dissent ought to be defended as a crucial element in the democratic process. We need to keep its opinions being heard across all areas of our culture, instead of being demonised. The politics of dissent very much needs to be addressed.

The anti-dissent imperative

There are various forces and conventions that are out to prevent us from expressing dissent. To demonstrate how widespread the anti-dissent imperative now is, I will work my way through a range of these over the course of this book. As a preview for what is to follow, it is noticeable how many governments have exploited populist sympathies to marginalise their political opponents. In the process they have done their best to make opposition seem unpatriotic, a charge that the left has struggled to defend itself against. Both the Trump and Johnson administrations can be cited in this regard. They are just as intolerant of dissenting views from within their own party as well: it does not pay to disagree with an anti-dissenter. The pandemic has provided cover for many governments to cut down opportunities to express political opposition, claiming this hampers their efforts to deal with Covid. Such a cynical use of Covid will feature prominently in my argument, since its effects are still very much with us. The pandemic has also been fertile ground for the growth of conspiracy theories, which social media have relentlessly promoted to a worldwide audience. Conspiracy theorists are dogmatists of the first order, unwilling to countenance other explanations than their own for events like the pandemic (or 9/11 or the Moon landings). Dissent yet again is marginalised by such beliefs, which does nothing for the cause of democratic public debate. Communism never had much time for dissent, but it is depressing to see it being attacked so systematically in the supposedly liberal democracies of the West.

Education is another area in which the right has been exerting itself of late. In America creationism is on the curriculum in many states as if it was an acceptable alternative to evolution theory. For the evangelical right, it is in fact the correct explanation of how humankind developed; evolutionists are there to be disproved. Then there are the activities of Turning Point USA and UK. These organisations encourage students to send in the names of teachers they feel are guilty of left-wing bias so they can be listed on their websites. The named teachers then find themselves exposed to attacks on social media (including death threats), all on the basis of anonymous accusations. Democratic debate gains nothing from this either.

How dissent fares under the various forms of democracy to be found on the contemporary political scene is another topic that invites close analysis. In Chapter 2, 'The State and Dissent', I examine the limits of democracy as a political system in detail. The invariably unhelpful attitude of the authorities to whistle-blowing soon makes such limits apparent, revealing a decidedly anti-democratic attitude to criticism on their part. Liberal democracy, with its regular elections and diversity of political parties, is designed to keep authoritarianism out of its governmental model. That is one of the features that differentiates it from the autocracies, theocracies and one-party states that are so prevalent in the non-Western world.

Yet even in a liberal democracy authoritarian rule is a constant threat. If a governing party has a large enough majority then it can in effect ignore dissenting voices: 'elective dictatorship', as it is known. That is the current state of affairs in the UK, with the Conservative majority at 83. But it could occur in any state using the 'first past the post' (FPTP) electoral model. Proportional representation is designed to resolve some of the problems associated with FPTP. It has two main types: 'alternative vote' and 'single transferrable vote', both of which can be adapted to local circumstances in terms of the weight given to transferred votes. 'Total representation' offers a hybrid of proportional and FPTP. None of these methods can guarantee that all votes count for the same, but they get closer to that ideal than UK elections do. As its supporters are quick to point out, however, FPTP is a more straightforward way of determining an election result.

Federalism introduces other factors into the electoral process, such as the relationship between central and regional government. There are many federal systems around the world and they take differing approaches to how they address this relationship. Each balances the power between its central and regional ruling bodies in its own particular way. As in proportional representation there is no perfect model and authoritarian outcomes are not unknown. The Trump presidency had distinctly autocratic tendencies, for example, as commentators like Masha Gessen have disapprovingly noted.[2] The populist-oriented white supremacist beliefs lying behind it have proved of particular concern to critics. Even though those beliefs spawned the Black Lives Matter movement in response, dissent faces some determined forces of suppression in the US. The central government–state government relationship can complicate this situation further. The American Senate is anything but a representative body, each state having two senators regardless of its population, and the discrepancy can be massive. California's population is more than sixty times that of Wyoming, skewing the centre–state balance of power in the latter's favour to an undemocratic degree. The EU is weighted towards its member states too, although in an even more radical way than in the US. As Brexit demonstrated, the EU allows members to opt out of its federal set-up if they disagree with how this is developing. The UK did so after the Leave campaign won the referendum, campaigning on the basis that EU membership was unduly curbing our national sovereignty. Having such a divorce clause (Article 50) built into the federation clearly limits the extent of central power. Yet it also introduces an element of instability in that other member states could take the same action, fragmenting the system. Anti-EU movements exist elsewhere in Europe and do pose something of a threat to the EU's longer-term prospects.

All the political systems above reveal that democracy has its limits, in that they can be manipulated in anti-democratic ways by unscrupulous politicians. Dissent's scope for expression is considerably reduced when that happens. When it comes to economic considerations, however, democracy is even more vulnerable and dissent even more constrained. Neoliberal economic theory, for example, involves a free-wheeling style of capitalism that widens the wealth gap in society to a degree that puts democracy at risk. It campaigns tirelessly against regulation by government, favouring as little intervention in the running of its affairs as possible. No matter how much influential economists complain about the growing wealth inequality that neoliberalism engenders, most Western governments are reluctant to rein it in.[3] It is difficult for dissent to make its voice heard here, except in the sense of campaigning about the adverse environmental impact of unrestricted capitalism. Extinction Rebellion is becoming ever more strident on that score, but the authorities have done their best to curtail its activities. Globalisation also plays its part in increasing wealth inequality in its commitment to outsourcing production from the West to cheaper labour markets in the developing world. Substantial job losses in the former have predictably followed. While this has led to some improvement in the economies of the new production centres, it has largely benefitted the owners rather than their workers. In countries like that, dissent tends to be severely suppressed as well.

Dissent also finds itself very restricted in the military, where obedience to one's superiors takes precedence over matters of conscience. Following orders blindly can, however, have unfortunate consequences, as the incidence of war crimes illustrates. There are some depressing examples of this to consider in modern times, most notably that of the Nazis. It is an interesting question how far one can go with what is an undoubted limit to democratic principles. Conscientious objection offers one way out in a democracy, but it is hardly encouraged.

Totalising theories are traditionally inimical to dissent from within their ranks, as both Marxism and the major monotheistic religions provide ample evidence for. To dissent from core doctrine is to declare yourself a heretic and to incur the wrath of the relevant authorities. I explore historical examples of how such heresies have been treated, as in the case of the Cathars, the Lollards and the Hussites. All these movements prefigured what we might now call a successful heresy in the form of Protestantism. The latter, however, turned just as authoritarian in its way and as intolerant of deviations from doctrine as Catholicism had been before it. It is striking to observe how far believers were willing to go to avoid falling into heresy (or what they thought of as such). John Bunyan's monumental psychological battle to overcome his fear of being too great a sinner to merit salvation, as recorded in his autobiography, provides an outstanding example.[4] Authority has to be totally obeyed from such a perspective, which makes it interesting to compare religion with the way that science has developed. Modern-day science views all theories as provisional: that is, valid only until some better explanation comes along, at which point the existing theory gives way to the new. Neither religions nor totalising ideologies tend to be as accommodating.

Turn to the arts and dissent can find itself just as unpopular amongst the establishment in the field. The arts have their own versions of totalising theories, as well as authority figures who do not like to be questioned. Modernism's rejection of tradition led its practitioners to view their peers who did not join them as lacking in imagination and stuck in the past. There was a certain arrogance about the movement that meant it looked down on its audience if they did not follow their highly experimental approach. Once again it was a case of there being thought to be only one way of doing things, that classic feature of totalising theories throughout history. Postmodernism went on to reject modernism and to resurrect a dialogue with the past. But it could be just as critical of those who did not follow its new creative model, just as resistant to dissent.

Ultimately, dissent is something that has to come from within each of us as individuals. I am therefore recommending that we make it a priority to develop internal systems to combat our own prejudices. Any of us can fail the 'woke test' on occasion and discriminate against others' beliefs. We should be subjecting our opinions to constant self-analysis, becoming as skilled as we can in the art of self-critique. Not, however, in the way that religions or totalising ideologies like communism tend to demand. In both of these, individuals are required to analyse their beliefs against the system's doctrines. The belief system itself is taken to be beyond criticism. Self-critique under these circumstances turns into a test of faith rather than of the theory in question's validity, as it manifestly did with Bunyan. Doubt about doctrine is not acceptable, whereas I regard it as an essential part of an anti-authoritarian personality.

All the topics and themes above will be dealt with in detail in what follows. The reader will have picked up by now that totalising theories constitute one of the book's major targets. They promote prejudice and bigotry and are to be avoided as much as possible. Overall, I will be encouraging a sceptical attitude towards authority and arguing that we should all be working to develop this on a personal level. The goal is to be motivated to confront authoritarianism and totalising theories in general, wherever we come across them.

Terminology

Before going on to the main argument itself, a brief word about terminology is called for. The concepts of dissent and opposition can be differentiated, as Ronald Collins and David Skover have done in their book *On Dissent*. They put the case for greater precision in our use of such terms, emphasising 'the need to be more clear-minded about this phenomenon we call dissent'.[5] But increasingly the two concepts are being conflated in popular usage – as in most media reporting. I will adopt that practice, on the principle that *all* opposition is being seen as dissent by authoritarian regimes. For such bodies, parliamentary opposition is no better than a street protest and social conscience a mere nuisance to be brushed aside. If you cannot accept that worldview and the loss of personal liberty and human rights it entails, then you define yourself as a dissenter. I hope readers of this study will feel persuaded to do so by its end.

Notes

1. See Brown, *In the Ruins of Neoliberalism*.
2. See Gessen, *Surviving Autocracy*.
3. See, for example, Piketty, *Capital in the Twenty-First Century*, for an in-depth critique of neoliberal theory.
4. See Bunyan, *Grace Abounding to the Chief of Sinners*.
5. Collins and Skover, *On Dissent*, p. xx.

Chapter 1

Dissent under Threat

Dissent is currently under systematic attack across the political spectrum, with governments globally increasingly trying to curtail opposition to their policies from either their political adversaries or the public realm in general. Ideological authoritarianism is very much on the rise and in the process dogmatism, prejudice and bigotry are playing an ever greater role in public life. The signs of this cultural shift have been building up steadily for some time now and we cannot assume it is a mere passing trend: it needs to be confronted now and with a sense of urgency. Donald Trump may have been voted out of office, but the ideas he stood for are still in circulation and maintaining their hold on his large support base. There is a politics of dissent and at the moment it has been taken over by the autocratically minded and exploited for their own devious purposes: it should be about scrutiny of authority, not suppression by it; frank debate and constructive criticism of authority's actions rather than uncritical belief that licenses them to do whatever they want and to refuse even to listen to the arguments of others. This situation raises a series of questions that will be addressed over the course of this book's argument:

- Why is dissent necessary?
- Why is dissent being opposed?
- Who gains from that policy and why?

- Where should dissent be encouraged and implemented?
- What can we do individually to aid the cause of dissent?

With these in mind, this first chapter will go on to consider the various ways in which dissent is currently under threat in contemporary society.

The turn against dissent

What is most striking about the turn against dissent that we are currently witnessing is the way that it has become so widespread in Western democracy, constituting a serious threat to its ideal of the free and open exchange of opposing political outlooks that is so basic to that system. Roland Bleiker sees modern-day dissent as a 'transnational phenomenon' that can resonate globally, but so is the turn against dissent and none of us is safe from its reach and its lack of qualms about doing whatever it takes to assert itself: ruthlessness is built into its calculations.[1] Ben Dorfman has pointed out that 'regardless of where one looks on historical bases as well as in times we might call our own, dissent has presence', but ensuring that that presence has the space and opportunity to make its views widely known is proving more and more difficult in contemporary life.[2] There has been, as Cas Mudde notes, a 'mainstreaming and normalization of the far right in general, and the radical right in particular, in the twenty-first century' and the repercussions are concerning for anyone on the centre or left of the political spectrum.[3] Administrations such as those of Donald Trump and Boris Johnson (the 'blond bullies and bunglers behind the world's greatest democracies', in Pankaj Mishra's withering assessment[4]), for example, have targeted the judiciary and the media industry for being critical of their policies, dismissing them as little better than enemies of the state and seeking to bring them under their control. Lawyers have been singled out in the UK as well, for the apparent sin of representing refugees. Similar tactics have been applied in Russia, Hungary and Poland, and in several other countries around the world such as Brazil. Checks and balances to their exercise of power are considered unacceptable by those governments and the notion of opposition denigrated, even to the extent of eradicating dissenting voices within one's own political party, no matter how mild in tone they may be. Solidarity of belief is insisted upon and criticism outlawed within the ruling party set-up: to step out of line is to risk being ostracised by one's colleagues or hounded out of the party altogether, a serious situation for a career politician to have to face. Boris Johnson has been quite ruthless in purging the Conservative Party of MPs who oppose any of his policies (particularly on Brexit, that all-consuming issue of British politics since the referendum of 2016), and Donald Trump simply fired any of his staff who questioned his actions, even only recently appointed ones – right up to the very closing days of his presidency. In both cases that sent out a very clear message about the level of loyalty expected.

Although the Brexit campaign and the Trump presidency originally pitched themselves as dissenting movements against the establishment, both soon took on an authoritarian character that brooked no opposition, often defining it as treasonous and encouraging the development of a narrow-minded populism that is distorting the political process through its embittered intolerance. Populism disdains opposition – any opposition. Dissent, as a study published in the aftermath of the 9/11 attacks in America put it, can be a distinctly 'dangerous' activity to engage in, and it has become ever more so in the intervening years as the authoritarian impulse has grown increasingly confident in asserting itself.[5] Authoritarianism of this nature is at present particularly associated with right-wing governments, and the resurgence in Europe and elsewhere of far-right politics, often with marked fascist characteristics, is beginning to pose a significant problem for liberal democratic polities. Right-wing populism is flourishing under such conditions and is having a profound effect on public debate, flooding social media with its bigotry and prejudices and creating an overall climate hostile to reasoned political debate. Social media is open to the left and centre as well as the right, of course, and Trump and Brexit have certainly generated a great deal of criticism there, as well as in the mainstream media. It has tended to be more diffuse than it is from the right, however, although clearly it played a role in Trump's defeat. Despite that, more people voted for Trump in 2020 than in 2016, meaning that his popularity amongst the electorate had actually increased, so some credit is due to social media campaigns on his behalf. How effective social media have been in influencing voters is difficult to pin down, but there is little doubt that they have helped to polarise political opinion to an alarming degree, particularly on the American scene. It has to be noted that Trumpism is alive and well and that Brexit is manifestly with us, hard evidence of just how successful right-wing extremism has been in setting the terms of contemporary political debate.

Dogmatic attitudes are becoming the order of the day under this dispensation, turning politics into an exercise in despair for many, on the left especially. What has been described as a 'left melancholia' can soon set in under these conditions and that has to be bad news for any liberal democracy, which thrives on diversity of opinion in the formal political sphere (although theorists such as Jacques Rancière, whose work will be considered in more detail in Chapter 2, take a more jaundiced view of the enterprise).[6] Chantal Mouffe has tried to be more positive than this, calling for a left populism to combat the right version.[7] But leaving aside for the moment whether more populism of any kind is desirable (it allows for little in the way of nuance after all, tending to homogenise political views), there is little evidence of this left populism emerging, mired as we are in what has been aptly described as a 'democratic recession'.[8] A recession, moreover, that gives every indication it is turning into a full-blown depression. Far too much of politics consists of appeals to prejudice and we slide ever further towards that state of depression every time these are made.

It has to be acknowledged that the left is just as capable of suppressing internal dissent as the right, yet again in the name of solidarity (the UK Labour Party's struggles with anti-Semitism in the last few years offering a very pertinent example on that score), and populism only too frequently exacerbates that tendency. I would argue that party unity is an overrated condition that holds back the cause of dissent, and without dissent you do not have a properly functioning democracy. It needs to be recognised as well that dissent within political parties is just as important to democracy as dissent from opposition forces without. Ideological positions constantly need to be reconsidered in the light of events, not taken as gospel; but it is the gospel supporters who are the ones throwing their weight around at present and endangering the stability of the entire system. The relationship between left and right, centre and right, is, to use Ian Leslie's term, 'conflicted', and the crackdown on dissent makes it all the more difficult to change minds on the other side, which Leslie, like Mouffe, argues is of paramount importance if we are to prevent further damage to the social fabric.[9] I agree wholeheartedly, but if we are not even allowed to voice dissent on politics as currently practised then we cannot get to the stage of trying to alter our adversary's mind, or doing our best to understand their point of view. That is the sad situation in which we now find ourselves. Recent worries that Western democracy might be drifting into a post-political state now need to be revised in the light of the concerted attempt by the right to take over the political in such a crude and unsubtle manner.[10] 'Post-political' is fast coming to mean being shut out of the decision-making political sphere by virulently anti-dissent extremists.

This study offers a robust defence of dissent, a polemic on its behalf, treating it as an essential part of any civilised society, without which that society is only too likely to ossify into an authoritarian, frequently totalitarian entity with minimal regard for human rights and civil liberties in general. Neither is this just a political issue: organisations in any area of activity are capable of developing in this manner, becoming intolerant of minority values and working to suppress opposition to their power so that they can act without restrictions. Corporate culture gravitates that way all too readily, managements always being keen to maximise the control they have over their workforce; hence the campaign they have so long waged against trade unions, with the effect that unions' influence has steadily deteriorated in the West over the last few decades to the point where they have little political impact any more and are ignored by most governments. Dissent is a necessary corrective to this cynical trait and its virtues need to be emphasised as strongly as possible, such that attempts to limit its ability to function are met with a principled resistance. George Orwell summed up the role of dissent very succinctly when he argued (in an unpublished preface to *Animal Farm*) that '[i]f liberty means anything at all, it means the right to tell people what they do not want to hear'.[11] Given that dissent has played such a vitally important role in the development of Western culture it will be considered in its widest sense, taking in philosophy, religion, the arts and sciences as well as politics, and drawing on key historical examples of it in action in all these areas to illustrate how it has helped to shape the modern world and its institutions. There are significant implications for the non-Western world in such an analysis too, given the high incidence there of one-party states, dictatorships and theocracies, which traditionally have been very severe on any expression of dissent as well as deeply suspicious of the concept of liberal democracy (or at best paying only lip-service to it, if it seems politically expedient to be seen to be doing so on the international stage).

Dissent has to be regarded as a key element in the struggle against dogmatic politics whatever its ideological orientation, a way to keep a politics of despair at bay. It should be thought of as a project against the authoritarian mentality and that is how it will be treated here, as a call to develop a dissenting personality with an appropriately sceptical attitude towards power and those who wield it. It is a project, furthermore, that anyone can contribute to, no matter what their position in society may be (a point made by Michel de Certeau in the past, but one that has taken on an air of greater urgency as a result of recent events[12]). Dissent is a state of mind that any of us can cultivate and apply in our own dealings with authority – supporting the aims of anti-racist movements such as Black Lives Matter, for example, which are showing up the shortcomings of officialdom everywhere over this issue, or those of Extinction Rebellion in its campaign against continued inaction by politicians on climate change. What that process also requires is to differentiate between what does and does not qualify as dissent, and that will be a critical part of this study overall, starting later in this chapter. Orwell, too, was concerned to make such a distinction:

> If the intellectual liberty which without a doubt has been one of
> the distinguishing marks of Western civilization means anything

at all, it means that everyone shall have the right to say and to print what he believes to be the truth, provided only that it does not harm the rest of the community in some quite unmistakeable way.[13]

Causing harm can never be an objective of dissent; it is, rather, a reason for dissent to go into action and make public its opposition to any such attempt – and in the contemporary political situation there are a host of these to be dealt with, as I will go on to outline.

Authoritarianism East and West

We became used to the authoritarian style of communist regimes over the history of Soviet communism, which has left a legacy of that style in the non-communist Russian state that emerged after its downfall in the 1990s. As it stands, Russia is little better than a travesty of democracy, without properly free elections or oppositional politics, where dissenting voices are ruthlessly quashed by an autocratic and distinctly oligarch-friendly leadership. A suspicious number of opponents of President Putin have been poisoned, for example: yet another very clear message about the level of loyalty expected to one's leaders. The Soviet period and the Tsarist regime before it have left little in the way of democratic principles behind them, with the result that Russians in general have never known anything very different politically speaking and are more or less resigned to it by now. The authoritarian imperative has survived as well in the old Soviet satellite states of the Cold War era in eastern Europe, most notably in the case of Poland and Hungary. There, human rights have been curtailed quite sharply and opposition systematically marginalised and victimised, despite the fact that this puts them at odds with their other partners in the EU, whose complaints over this manifestly anti-democratic behaviour have been largely ignored to date. As with the Soviet Union, the lack of any recent history of democratic politics has made it easier for the governments to close down opposition, and any that exists has to proceed with the utmost care, knowing how little respect for civil liberties and human rights their governmental machine has.

Opposition is not for the faint-hearted in such cases, where it can often lead to prison or forced exile (sometimes even death, as with the dissident Saudi Arabian journalist Jamal Khashoggi, murdered in his country's consulate in Istanbul in 2019 in a graphic illustration of autocracy's utter disregard for public opinion).

China has kept up the tradition of authoritarian communism and its contempt for dissent, as pioneered by the Soviet Union, regarding almost any opposition to the Party's policies as treasonous – as the residents of Hong Kong have been finding out to their cost in recent years, their promised freedoms in the aftermath of British colonial rule, under their own elected ruling council, being progressively curbed to the point where they mean very little at all any more. Lockdowns, in the form of curfews, were occurring periodically in Hong Kong even before the pandemic struck, the target being street protests calling for a more democratic political set-up; these were brutally put down by the authorities, acting as directed by the central government in Beijing. Resistance from the Uighurs has been summarily quashed by the Chinese government as well and Tibet remains a source of disquiet under Chinese occupation. It may have permitted a certain amount of capitalist enterprise to exist in the country, a pragmatic move to boost the economy and make it competitive internationally, but there is no doubt that the Chinese Communist Party (CCP) is in complete control of Chinese life and dictates what happens there; if capitalism exists, then it is on the terms of the Party. The CCP is the sole legal political organisation in the country and gives little indication it has any intention of altering that system; political debate, such as it is, has to take place within the Party itself, which is highly secretive about such matters (as communist parties traditionally have been), always concerned to present a face of unity to the world.

Liberal democracy has been more common in the Western world, but dissent has been a significant factor in the non-Western too, as the continuing protests in Hong Kong demonstrate. The 'Arab Spring' was an example of a simmering dissent in the Islamic world, which is traditionally inimical to that phenomenon, and it is still there despite heavy-handed government crackdowns in response – the 'Arab Winter' as it has come to be called.[14] Asef

Bayat finds hopeful signs in the 'unconventional forms of agency and activism [that] have emerged in the region', whereby Arab populations can express their political agency at the everyday level in what he dubs 'social nonmovements'.[15] These go to make up a 'street politics' of daily life, where individuals can exchange views about the authorities, thus keeping a spirit of dissent alive.[16] While that is good to hear, it has to be noted that the regimes in question are still in control, several years after Bayat's book came out. Then there is the long-running tragic saga of the Palestinian people, whose dissent against their loss of territory as a result of the creation of the state of Israel in 1948 has drawn a harsher and harsher reaction from the Israeli authorities down the years. Not harsh enough, however, to prevent dissent from continuing to flare up. Dissent can and does arise in all political systems, therefore, irrespective of their ideological orientation, with street protests and civil disobedience expressing deep public frustration about the failings of the authorities (and being strongly defended as a democratic right by such as Hannah Arendt).[17] Authoritarianism can and does arise in all political systems too and the focus of my argument in this study is on how that tendency can be countered. What we desperately need now is a mainstreaming and normali-sation of dissent throughout all political systems, both in the East and in the West; a vastly increased presence that can be neither ignored nor closed down by antagonistic authorities. The Trump presidency certainly qualified as the latter, with Masha Gessen arguing that it 'had come closer to achieving autocratic rule than most people would have thought possible'.[18] The fact that this could happen in the leading nation in the West, one that has tra-ditionally seen itself as a model of democratic principle for the rest of the world, ought to make us very aware of the scale of the task that dissent currently finds itself confronted by.

Most of the examples of anti-authoritarian dissent over the course of this book will come from the West, because that is the area where the suppression of dissent by anti-democratic forces has been most evident of late (and the one I am assuming readers will be most familiar with too). Liberal democracy posits an insti-tutional role for dissent so it becomes all the more obvious when this is being curbed or even outlawed. The Western bias is meant not to undervalue the many struggles being waged against authoritarianism throughout the rest of the world, but to indicate that we should never take dissent for granted. Even in systems that claim to be models of democratic conduct for others to follow, dissent is a vulnerable phenomenon in need of careful guarding; without it, the pluralism on which liberal democracy crucially depends will be stifled. It is the sinister and widespread efforts with that end in mind that have generated the writing of this book.

Public crises, emergency powers and dissent

Public crises, such as the coronavirus pandemic of 2020, pose yet another threat to the expression of dissent, both within liberal democracies and within more autocratically inclined regimes. There is no doubt that the way the coronavirus pandemic has been handled has contributed to the spread of authoritarianism. Many national governments assumed emergency powers, effectively shutting down normal political life and making it very difficult to scrutinise any action they undertook. The crisis was taken to be significant enough justification for the suspension of civil liberties that resulted, as in the many lockdowns that were instituted, closing businesses and limiting individual movement – backed up by varying degrees of police enforcement to ensure compliance (more in China, predictably, given the control exercised by the CCP). Calling it a 'war' against the virus, as most governments did, helped to legitimate the imposition of such measures, war traditionally leading to far greater state control over its citizens (and war can be declared on just about anything politicians want these days, from drugs and crime through to health emergencies, a point I will be returning to below). The closure of many national parliamentary bodies further hampered opposition and in that sense could be seen as a gift to almost any government, since ministers could not be put on the spot, or caught out, by opponents' questions in open debate: scrutiny at a distance loses much of its impact and is far easier for government officials to deal with. Any such increase in central government control has to be viewed with considerable apprehension, however, since it is only too easy to abuse the absolute power that it grants and to dismiss dissent as unpatriotic – a tactic the political right has little hesitation in calling upon, time after time. For people on the far right in particular, they are the only true patriots; no-one else can be trusted. To question government policy, even mildly, can be made to look close to treason (the Chinese are quite blatant about this, punishing transgressors severely). The emergency is designed to sideline opposition, leaving the government with a free hand; in this it has been broadly successful.

Dissent has a hard enough time making its views public in autocratic societies anyway, governments there having no reservations about using the police and the military to enforce their political will; but the advent of a crisis is a very convenient excuse to crack down further and it sets a pattern which can be hard to break even when the crisis passes. Liberal democracies can be caught out in this way as well; Brexit, for example, was treated as enough of a crisis by a newly elected prime minister, Boris Johnson, for him to suspend Parliament for several weeks in 2019 to prevent it blocking his plans. Precedents like that are troubling in a liberal democracy, especially one like the UK where the (unwritten) constitution is so heavily based on custom and practice. Crude though the move was (and illegal, as it was subsequently judged to be by the UK's Supreme Court), it was also highly effective, as is likely to be noted by future ruling parties looking for ways out of awkward situations.

The Cambodian government was quick off the mark in taking advantage of the coronavirus pandemic, passing legislation by April 2020 that authorised it to implement an alarmingly wide-ranging set of emergency powers in the event of anything that it deemed to be a crisis. It was to be the sole arbiter in the latter respect, wording the legislation vaguely enough to make this as easy as possible for its leaders to claim. No opposition to its decision was to be permitted either, with appropriately harsh penalties drawn up to punish anyone brave enough, or rash enough, to make such an attempt. Dissent was more or less declared illegal under this system. The Philippine government went so far as to direct its police force to shoot to kill if anyone was caught deliberately breaking any of the emergency measures it had put in place: not much room allowed for dialogue there. Neither government had been particularly democratic in spirit beforehand and had never had much patience with dissent, but the pandemic presented all the justification they required to abandon even the pretence of being so. To pre-empt criticism they could even claim that it was in the public interest for them to act in this way, because it made it easier to take prompt action to protect their citizens. Any opposition at all to the government's policies could be labelled a crisis and used as a pretext to increase its powers further and to extend them indefinitely into the future. All of this was apparently legal, thus making dissent's task all the more arduous. An opportunity to bypass democratic norms will always be welcomed by authoritarians, who will do their utmost to avoid accountability, a condition they consider themselves to be beyond.

Emergency powers can be notoriously difficult to end; crises of one kind or another are a standard part of human existence after all (especially if it is those in power who are deciding what qualifies as one, as they are so frequently doing already with the notion of 'war'), and governments can become quite addicted to them. Absolute power is rarely given up voluntarily; more often than not it requires a revolution to remove it – and more often than not it has to be a violent one, taking us into the area of resistance explored by Howard Caygill, when open defiance of the authorities comes into play. For Caygill, '[t]he most pervasive framing discourse of resistance is *force*', with both sides resorting to that in a bid to overcome the other.[19] While a violent revolution clearly constitutes a massive show of dissent, and as Barbara J. Falk reminds us, historically speaking it 'remains difficult to separate dissent from violence', it has to be considered a desperate method of expressing it.[20] Judith Butler also notes 'a link between dissent and the right to revolution', but a society where dissent is not suppressed but is free to make its case without fear of official reprisal is far preferable to one that requires a bloody revolution.[21] Just to clarify my own position on the matter, it will be dissent in its non-violent form that I will be defending throughout this book, arguing for a greater presence of it in all our affairs. On that basis, plus given its firmly anti-authoritarian bias and sceptical outlook, I feel I can use the term 'dissent' to cover a wider range of activities and responses than was the case with the commentators referred to in the Introduction, Ronald Collins and David Skover.[22] Not all forms of opposition will meet those criteria, so these provisos provide adequate scope for discrimination as to what should count as dissent and thus can be supported by us with a clear conscience.

EU states such as Hungary have also interpreted the pandemic as an opportunity to extend government control dramatically, with the same worry arising as to when, or if, they will cut this back: an exit strategy is not always built into such moves, quite deliberately, one has to conclude. In Russia, too, the government took a tough line with opposition to the lockdown and anyone found guilty of breaking its conditions. Governments with autocratic pretensions exploited the pandemic as much as they could, regarding it as a welcome opportunity to marginalise dissent for the foreseeable future and thus render it extremely difficult to remove them from office (even in democracies there can be a hankering after the condition of being 'president for life' amongst its leaders, with Donald Trump for one expressing interest in the notion while still in office). The opportunity to accuse dissenters of being unpatriotic or treasonous has been seized on by what one could call the usual suspects, and it does not bode well for the development of political life in any of the nations in question. One-party, strong-leader politics beckons when dissent is subjected to such treatment – and exit strategies are not generally built into these phenomena either.

Culture war

As noted above, the use of the term 'war' has become ubiquitous in political life globally, and it has come to a head in the West of late with the right's insistence that it is engaged in a 'culture war' with its political opponents. The phrase could just be dismissed as mere rhetoric, but it is insidious in its implications. War is about overcoming your enemies and leaving them unable to continue opposing you, not just about winning an argument. The Nazi Party was not allowed to go on ruling Germany after its defeat in the Second World War; it was abolished and made illegal. When the right says it is in a culture war against anyone with liberal views (which takes in both the political centre and left, even some on the non-extreme right), then it is expressing similar sentiments; it does not simply want to win the argument, it wants to render it impossible for such views to be expressed at all and for the institutions that propagate them to be neutered or closed down altogether. That is not how democratic political life is supposed to work and it indicates an ultra-authoritarian state of mind of the kind that we would expect to find in a one-party state, not a liberal democracy. The right's goal is to be more than just the dominant culture in its nation, it is to be the only permitted culture; it is no fan of intellectual liberty, or difference or diversity of outlook. It was dismaying to hear that line of argument coming from an American president in the case of Donald Trump, especially when it was directed at institutions such as the press and the university system, where freedom of expression is vital to their integrity. It is total control over discourse that is being sought and that is precisely what dissent sets itself in opposition to. Not all on the right are so undemocratic, but the more they align themselves with the far right then the more they merit that description, and unfortunately that is the way politics appears to be developing in too many instances (as the current travails of the American Republican party signal only too clearly). It is the far right that is setting the tone of debate more than is comfortable at present, aiming unapologetically at dominating proceedings and imposing its ideology on its society.

The left has to be careful not to be drawn into this way of thinking, which gives a false picture of what democratic political debate should be. It merely entrenches the notion that political opponents are to be considered enemies, there to be removed from the political scene by whatever means necessary; debate as such does not come into it. That leads to a culture of intolerance which narrows the scope for dissent quite drastically and the far left can often mirror the far right in taking up such a position, commandeering public discourse for its own exclusive use (communism was completely open about doing this, which ought to stand as a permanent warning to the left, which is prone, rather too conveniently, to forget that aspect of its history). Attitudes harden on both sides of the ideological divide when that happens and political parties and their supporters become less and less inclined to acknowledge any merit at all in opposing viewpoints, or to be minded towards any compromise or constructive dialogue with them, which is the situation we are repeatedly finding ourselves in nowadays. Claiming to be in a culture war sends out all the wrong signals, effectively outlawing dissent; it could be summed up by saying that if culture war means anything, it means a war against dissent.

Conspiracy theory and dissent

Public crises give rise to yet another tricky issue concerning dissent and what deserves to qualify as that: the attraction they hold for conspiracy theorists, who very quickly latch on to these events as opportunities to lecture the rest of us on their 'real' causes – which only they seem to be in the know about. The coronavirus pandemic generated its share of these, particularly the theory, widely propagated on social media, a natural home for conspiracy theorists, that it was the installation of the 5G telecommunications network around the world that was the main reason for its rapid spread. The 3G and 4G networks had been similarly accused of previous disease outbreaks when they came on stream, so there is a conspiracy history to build on here, which will no doubt be accessed again in any future technological update; conspiracy never seems to go out of fashion. Groups such as 'Stop 5G UK' and 'Destroy 5G Save Our Children' were soon in operation and gaining significant support amongst the social media community. Arson attacks on 5G masts in the UK were one consequence of this belief, which no amount of condemnation by major political figures seemed able to quell. In fact, denial by politicians merely served to fuel the theory, the claim being that they were obviously trying to deflect attention from their own part in the conspiracy. The theorists were clearly disagreeing with the official line on the pandemic and on the face of it that could be described as an incidence of dissent, although it could only count as socially valuable dissent if there was any truth behind its belief, which does not exist in this case (nor did it with 3G or 4G). Indeed, the explanations for the link all sound rather like a science fiction film, and a cliched one at that, involving waves being emitted by the network's infrastructure that weaken the human immune system and make it easier for the microbe to invade it. No medical evidence whatsoever exists for this belief, but that would never deter the committed conspiracy believer, for whom that can only mean it is being hidden by those behind the conspiracy. No-one suspends disbelief quite so willingly (and rigorously) as the conspiracy follower.

The situation with 5G is reminiscent of what has happened with the theory of creationism, which dates the age of the Earth from the information given in the Bible, making it roughly 8,000 years old as opposed to the several billion that science records. Although there is no scientific evidence at all for creationist theory, it is taken seriously enough by its adherents for them to have succeeded in getting it on to the school curriculum in many American states (as well as in some faith-based schools in the UK) as if it was an intellectually credible rival to the scientific account, to be taught so that individuals can make up their own minds as to which they find the better. 'The jury is still out on that' was a line of argument often put forward to justify this action: President George W. Bush even used it when queried on his beliefs. The 5G conspiracy has been taken up by some in the media on the same basis, as a theory that deserves to be considered as valid as the scientific explanations (every incidence of which seems to provoke more arson attacks on phone masts). It has now reached a level of credibility with some, helped on by the celebrity endorsement that so often occurs in these cases, that bears no resemblance to the available evidence – or lack of it, to put it more bluntly.

There are other theories also popping up on social media about the cause of Covid-19, such as it having been deliberately created and spread by governments in an attempt to reduce the world's population so as to bring down the rate of carbon emissions. Another claim is that the virus was manufactured by the Chinese government as part of a plan to transform itself into the dominant force in the world, a theory which went down particularly well in the US. President Trump claimed it could be traced back to a virology laboratory in Wuhan, the original source of the pandemic (although other sources have since been suggested for this, including some outside China), another display of his talent at what has been scathingly referred to as 'policy-based evidence-making'. A more plausible suggestion put forward by some was that it was an 'accident' that the virus had escaped from the laboratory, but as of the time I write there is no proof for this either. Why China would choose to release it first on its own citizens has to remain something of a mystery; but conspiracy theorists can always argue their way around inconsistencies. A cunning ploy by the Chinese authorities to disguise their complicity perhaps? (One cannot imagine conspiracists believing in anything as mundane as an 'accident' as a cause either; there seem to be no such things in their world, which is a network of dark and devious plots.) The notion of governments acting in such a deeply unethical, indeed outright inhuman, manner as this was also promoted during the AIDS epidemic back in the 1980s, and those who mistrust governments can always be found to build up a following for such ideas, no matter how far-fetched and fantastical they may be. Even though governments have been known to act in unethical and inhuman ways in the past, really substantial proof would be needed to back up such notions as the above in our own day and for the particular reasons given. Sadly, not every member of the public seems to believe this is necessary; their feeling instead is that somebody must be to blame and not just microbes, conveniently forgetting that the latter require no human help at all to go about their business of undermining people's health. If anything is seeking world domination it is the empire of Microbia, and we can be sure that Covid will not be its last shot at this. No amount of policy-based evidence-making will have any effect on the phenomenon either.

Nearly every public crisis spawns conspiracy theories (9/11 produced a slew of these, which are still in circulation to this day) and they are notoriously difficult to respond to, because to challenge them immediately turns you into part of the conspiracy in the eyes of most true believers – or at best shows you up as naive about what the powerful are capable of sanctioning. Conspiracy theories cannot, however, be considered to qualify as dissent as it is understood here in this study. They may be oppositional and directed against authority, but they are based on unsubstantiated assumptions which do not bear much examination; if anything, they are closer to dogmatism than dissent, since they are all but impervious to proof to the contrary – a suitable case for scepticism if there ever was one. True believers think proof that they are right is being kept from them by unscrupulous forces and they are not open to debate about such things, whereas real dissenters always are. Dissent can justify itself in a way that conspiracy cannot. The sceptical spirit is one of the main drivers of dissent, whereas it is foreign to the outlook of the confirmed conspiracy theorist, and it will inform the approach I will be taking for the rest of this book.

The scientific spirit is foreign to the conspiracy theorist too. Scientists are committed to constant testing of their theories and are prepared to ditch them (or at the very least, significantly to rework them) if the testing reveals really significant anomalies, or suggests that new lines of enquiry might be more fruitful. Conspiracists, however, look for confirmation of their theory and avoid testing it in the manner of a scientist or a sceptic; the theory is there to be reinforced only, a constant factor that is considered to be beyond doubt and dissent. Their theory is a prejudice in favour of one explanation of events at the expense of all others – and prejudice tends to dig in for the long term. This is the opposite of scientific method, which, as I shall be discussing in more detail in Chapter 5, is based on provisionality; on theories always being subject to revision, or replacement, if another theory proves to be more reliable. They are both dependent on evidence, but how they compile and select it differs enormously – as does what they go on to do with it.

The anti-vaccination movement provides yet another example of how dogmatism can come to undermine the struggle against health crises. Vaccination is designed to combat disease and has been successfully doing so since it was first developed in the eighteenth century; but because of some very problematic research postulating a connection between measles-mumps-rubella (MMR) vaccination and autism, published in 1998, long since discredited by the relevant medical authorities, the anti-vax movement has gained a substantial following who regard vaccination as a dangerous practice that threatens rather than safeguards their health.[23] Anti-vaccination material is widely available across social media and its impact is becoming a cause for concern in an era suffering through a pandemic: street protests against vaccination are becoming frequent events that draw a lot of news coverage, as well as free publicity for the campaign, which will only make the virus all the harder to eradicate now that vaccines are widely available. As the medical profession keeps pointing out, a society with Covid-spreaders circulating freely in it after a vaccine has been introduced is not going to be an entirely safe one, but anti-vaxxers are impervious to such arguments. Once again, as with the 5G protests, what appears to be dissent against authority is seen to be something more sinister, as well as deeply irrational, with vaccination being treated as yet one more in a long line of conspiracies hatched by the powers-that-be, who would seem to spend their time doing little else. (Cass R. Sunstein has rather drily noted that 'conspiracy theorists typically overestimate the competence and discretion of officials and bureaucracies, which are assumed to be capable of devising and carrying out sophisticated secret plans'.[24] Anyone who has followed the bungled handling of the pandemic by so many national governments will be alive to the irony of such assumptions. The fiasco over deciding what was permissible in the way of Christmas celebrations in the UK in 2020 stands as a glaring example of just how inept government planning can be. Large-scale conspiracies would need an almost superhuman level of control to prevent leaks or mistakes from occurring and even the most autocratic of governments will struggle to achieve that condition indefinitely.) It is not scepticism that is in operation in such cases, it is merely prejudice, often based on what Heidi J. Larson has referred to as 'deep-rooted angers against the state' that vaccination merely brings to a head, and it should never be confused with dissent.[25] There are, as she also somewhat pessimistically notes, 'new notions of "evidence" taking hold' amongst a significant section of the populace, largely derived from social media postings, that are going to continue posing problems for those trying to combat disease outbreaks – regardless of how sincere their efforts might be.[26] There is in effect a pandemic of anti-vaxxers around at the moment and it looks set to outlast Covid-19, especially since it includes some prominent serving politicians in its ranks around the globe. Prejudice has a wide reach.

This is fast turning into a golden age for conspiracy theories, the latest to appear as I write being QAnon, which came to prominence trading on the idea that a globally organised 'deep state' of elites was working away behind the scenes to try and bring down the Trump presidency. Unsurprisingly, the 2020 presidential election result was pounced on by believers as proof that this had to be true; they would accept no other explanation for their hero having lost. QAnon has a substantial presence on the net – that almost goes without saying for conspiracy theories these days – and was endorsed by none other than Trump himself at a press conference: 'I don't know much about the movement other than I understand they like me very much, which I appreciate' (a statement which becomes more worrying the more you think about it).[27] The protagonists in this deep state are the usual shadowy hordes of Satanists, paedophiles and child-sex traffickers, who can always be called on by conspiracy theorists to justify their campaign (those involved in the Pizzagate scandal during Hillary Clinton's campaign in the 2016 presidential election against Trump made much the same accusations). It is, as Richard Scorer has rightly noted in an analysis of QAnon's activities, a 'ludicrous theory', but it has nevertheless caught on to the extent that child protection agencies in America are beginning to complain that it is having an adverse effect on their work.[28] Trump's tacit endorsement meant that anyone who opposed him in any way was by implication a supporter of this deep state, so dissent is by definition suspect – a useful tactic for him to deploy in an election year, helping to make it one of the most chaotic in American history. The notion that opposing a head of state, even if this is just standing against him in an election (and for a reputable political party), is a sign of evil intent, is just about as far away from democracy as one would ever want to be.

Another case of dissent under attack at present in 2021 is to be found in Belarus, where President Lukashenko, often referred to as the last dictator in Europe, treats opposition to him as a crime, as a result of which opposition politicians have been arrested, with others fleeing into exile to escape that fate. The apparent rigging of the country's last presidential election prompted huge street protests, drawing the usual claims of being part of a conspiracy against the state, and were met with a predictably violent response by police and a flurry of arrests. Even if Lukashenko's regime were to be brought down, what is sobering to note is that similar cases just keep on cropping up, making them symbolic of the way that dissent is steadily being driven out of the political arena. Conspiracy theory is becoming a major factor in this process and it can be turned to account by any authoritarian regime looking for scapegoats (as anti-Semitism has been so often in the past). A golden age for conspiracy theory is anything but for democracy. Just to give us further pause as to the extent of the problem, Sunstein has suggested that 'conspiracy theorizing is, in a sense, built into the human condition', and, even more ominously, that any of us is capable of succumbing to the lure of our 'inner conspiracy theorist, at least on occasion'.[29] How we might resist that lure, developing our inner dissenter instead, will be one of the topics discussed in Chapter 7.

QAnon has extended its reach to the field of science, claiming that both Covid-19 and climate change are conspiracies. As one commentator observed in 2020: 'QAnon hasn't just cornered the market in conspiracy theories, but is morphing into a conspiracy-industrial complex of reality denial that threatens to sway the most important US general election since the last one' (a statement that might well apply in the next, too).[30] Even if it did not manage to sway it enough, that there is such a ready market for 'reality denial' is the saddest part of this situation. Conspiracy seems well on the way to becoming one of the most popular ideologies of our time, vigorously mainstreamed and normalised to the point where it is practically attaining the status of a new world religion (perhaps Trump can be dubbed one of its patron saints). Dissent against this 'conspiracy-industrial complex' is simply denied to have any basis whatsoever in reality.

Right-wing dissent, higher education and bigotry

A particularly insidious example of how right-wing dissent can present serious problems for freedom of speech can be found in the campaigns being run by the educational pressure groups Turning Point USA and Turning Point UK.[31] The latter, echoing its American parent, describes itself on its website as 'a grassroots organisation dedicated to educating students and other young people on the values of free markets, limited government and personal responsibility', all fairly standard right-wing ideals.[32] Those values are to be defended 'against a dogmatic Left-wing political climate, education system and radical Labour Party', although that 'Left-wing political climate' may have escaped many of us in the UK after more than a decade of Conservative Party rule and an 83-strong majority in place for the current government. It is ironic also that the pandemic has made a very persuasive case for strong rather than limited government, given the scale of the social problems it has created. States which have tried to hold to the limited-government ethos, where individuals are thrown back on their own resources to deal with any problems that come their way, have been the ones to suffer worst from the pandemic (the US and Brazil, most notably, where limited government has come to mean limited access to affordable healthcare, exacerbating the impact of the virus).

The point of the campaigns is to compile lists of the names of academics who express left-wing views in their teaching and then to publish them on their respective websites, Professor Watchlist and Education Watch. The former describes itself as being on a 'mission . . . to expose and document college professors who discriminate against conservative students and advance leftist propaganda in the classroom', and with a claimed 'presence on over 2,000 campuses' it is building up an impressive network for propagating its views: 'We play offense with a sense of urgency to win America's culture war,' as it proudly announces.[33] Education Watch proclaims that '[i]t's time to end the politicisation of our young people by people who should know better!'; as if teaching the young the 'values of free markets, limited government and personal responsibility' somehow or other did not constitute politicisation.[34] We are in culture war territory again here.

Students are encouraged by the websites to supply the names of lecturers whom they consider to be guilty of left-wing bias in their courses, anonymously if they wish. This amounts to an open invitation to anyone with a grudge; a poor essay grade would be enough justification for some to take up the offer and that puts all academics in the firing line. On that flimsy basis alone they are added to the list, with the only too predictable result that death threats have been issued online to some of those so named. Far-right extremism seems to regard the death threat as an entirely acceptable political tactic, to be applied against anyone expressing anything other than far-right extremist sentiments, and social media is always available to post these on (one of the most dramatic was the call by the ex-Trump advisor Steve Bannon for the beheading of the director of the FBI and America's top public health official; the problem always being with such rhetoric, even if only satirically intended – as one sincerely hopes this was – that it may persuade some deranged individual actually to attempt it). This is the right's version of cancel culture and it is on duty 24/7: so much for intellectual liberty.

The sites are based on the assumption that universities in both America and Britain are hotbeds of left-wing thought and that students will suffer if they are exposed to these, that they are in fact in danger of being brainwashed by unscrupulous left-wingers unless the latter are publicly shamed (one might wonder why there are so many right-wing governments around the world at present if the education system has been so hostile to their ideology and churning out so many indoctrinated left-wing zealots, but such campaigns are more interested in rhetoric than facts). The notion that the right should engage in debate with left-wing views if it disagrees with them rather than resort to censorship, or the death threat, is simply discounted. Freedom of speech is being put at risk by such campaigns (despite the American website's banner headline claim that 'We Believe in Freedom'[35]), which also have a particularly wide conception of what constitutes left-wing thought – being in favour of gender equality qualifies, for instance. It comes as no surprise to find that the Turning Point movement won the approval of President Trump and as American presidents effectively set the benchmark for national public discourse during their tenure in office, this lent their campaign an air of respectability (no surprise either to find that Nigel Farage is an enthusiastic supporter of the UK branch).

Turning Point appears to be a dissenting movement against intellectual authority as it is wielded in higher education, and all authority has to expect to be questioned in this way; no authority should ever be immune from this process of sceptically minded scrutiny, which works to keep it honest and not acting against the public interest. But in reality Turning Point wants to stamp out the possibility of any dissent at all against its own ideological position; anything that it deems to be left-wing is by definition wrong-headed, a remit which includes any viewpoint that differs from its own. 'We Believe in Freedom', but we decide what it means and what it allows: politicisation is what our opponents do, not us. Intolerance of other beliefs is the house style and even the suggestion of dissent is to be hunted down and silenced. That is not what scepticism is about; neither shaming nor death threats constitute philosophical moves. Universities where nothing but extreme right-wing views could be expressed or taught would not be universities, they would be propaganda machines better suited to the world of George Orwell's *1984* than that of pluralist liberal democracy. They would effectively be a mirror image of the university system under the Soviet regime. Naming and shaming as promoted by Turning Point raise the spectre of Big Brother and his all-seeing eye on the lookout for dissidents like Winston Smith, ready to crack down the minute they are found to have stepped out of line; all it takes is an anonymous complaint (fascist regimes encouraged a similar response from their citizens as to possible dissidents, even encouraging children to report their own parents). If nothing else, these watchlists may make academics more prone to self-censorship, which would represent a significant victory for the far right. Not everyone can be expected to deal with a death threat with equanimity; many will decide instead to keep their views to themselves and steer clear of saying anything even remotely ideologically contentious, choosing to suspend their political agency rather than expose themselves to risk. Silence equals an absence of dissent in such cases and the longer this goes on then the less it is apparent that there is anything wrong with the dominant set of values. Taking refuge in silence is one of the most insidious effects of the suppression of dissent and authoritarian regimes are well aware of how it works to their advantage; they can present it back to the electorate as consent if no-one is complaining to the contrary. Dissent is caught in a double bind at such points, because above all it wants to be recognised as legitimate, both in its formal and informal guises, not to be forced to hide; '[d]issent requires entering public space,' as Barbara Falk has summed it up.[36] Denial of such recognition, as Axel Honneth has pointed out, merely increases the social and political tensions in any nation by putting up barriers to the creation of social relationships based on mutual respect.[37]

It could be argued that right-wing watchlists constitute an understandable response to the no-platforming tactics directed against right-wing thinkers by so many universities, student groups and liberal-oriented public organisations, perhaps lending the lists a certain amount of legitimacy. No-platforming is a highly controversial issue and it has enabled the right to argue that it denies it freedom of speech, a not implausible claim. As Evan Smith has observed, 'the concept of free speech has been weaponised by the right in its various guises as a smokescreen to air offensiveness and to promulgate far right ideas about race, sexuality and gender'.[38] We are now caught up in 'free speech wars', as another study on the topic has described the situation, and it would have to be said that the right's tactics are proving to be the more successful to date.[39] Every example of no-platforming creates an opportunity for those on the right to cast themselves as martyrs, which can resonate with the wider public and gain them some sympathy in consequence; claiming to be defending freedom and personal responsibility sounds entirely in line with the spirit of democracy. Generally speaking, no-platforming's target is the expression of racist or misogynist views, which are often banned by law, although there is a grey area as to how these are interpreted, or expressed, as well as whether they should be censored or openly debated with in order to reveal their logical inconsistency (and the harm they can do). The political left and centre is very much divided on which is the best course of action to take, which is of course to the advantage of the right, since it can always claim that the left is being hypocritical in denying it the opportunity to express its views in public while ostensibly being in favour of freedom of speech itself. In situations like these the accusation of cancel culture is only too easy to make and increasingly is being resorted to by the apparently aggrieved right. The alt-right movement in America, for example, has found this to be a very effective method of berating the left, thus deflecting attention away from its own distinctly fascistic views and tactics. As commentators such as Mike Wendling have insisted, we should not allow ourselves to be taken in by this ploy: 'the argument that the alt-right represents a "counter-culture" comes almost entirely from the movement itself and rings hollow when properly examined'.[40] Which is to say that it cannot qualify as proper dissent.

What is really at issue here is whether freedom of speech should include the airing of prejudice in public places. There would quite probably be a majority in agreement in liberal democracies that it should not, but that merely raises the vexed issue of precisely what counts as a prejudiced viewpoint. It is not enough to say that it is one that breaks the law, because the law can be changed, each generation having a different opinion as to what constitutes prejudice (although that is not to say the law is always right; this was patently not the case with the anti-Semitic 'laws' passed by the Nazi government in the 1930s, and the harm that they did is unmistakable and unforgiveable). Nevertheless, a common element in prejudice over the ages is that it involves discrimination against specific, generally minority, groups, to the extent of sanctioning that reaction amongst the wider public.[41] Currently it is liberals who are being targeted and added to an infamous list that includes non-whites, Jews, and religious believers other than Christians (Muslims particularly). Hate speech against such groups is now a permanent feature of social media, where it finds a ready audience, bringing out latent prejudices only too successfully and considerably increasing the scale of the problem that liberal societies face. Those peddling hate speech can always find other users who 'like' their posts and are prepared to pass them on, building up a sense of being part of a community that has a real grievance to pursue; an attitude that can be hard to break.

Social media will probably remain a very difficult area to police, so we have to assume that hate speech will continue to be part of our culture until more sophisticated methods of preventing it

from spreading are devised. Also platform-owners need the will
to take action against it, which cannot be taken for granted given
the huge profits involved in their industry: turning a blind eye has
been more their style to date, or yet more dubious claims to be
defenders of freedom of speech. More to the point, however, would
be to address how hate speech comes into being in the first place
and try to work out ways of preventing that from happening, or at
the very least of reducing its incidence. Education is the obvious
place to start, and that would mean trying to ensure that students
reaching university would not be so open to the message of groups
like Turning Point, that they would recognise prejudice when they
saw it and refuse to support those peddling it. By all means teach
the values of the free market and capitalism, but also their flaws
and failings, as well as what their opponents argue would make for
a better, more egalitarian, economic and socio-political system.
Capitalism cannot be assumed to be an essential part of every
democracy, nor right-wing thought the only valid kind in the
political arena. Unfortunately, that is a view which is now becoming enshrined in government education policy in the UK, with
works that express anti-capitalist sentiments being removed from
the school curriculum. Given the considerable amount of literature that covers, by a renowned and prestigious cast of authors
(Charles Dickens was not exactly kind to capitalists in novels like
Hard Times, as just one notable example), this has to be seen as
a very worrying sign of what the authorities might be planning
in the longer term and to raise the issue of whether other parts
of the education system can expect the same treatment. Higher
education without such texts is almost unthinkable and the dread
spectre of censorship looms up. One wonders why, if capitalism is
thought to be so self-evidently the best basis for any political system, its supporters are so sensitive to contrary views and so wary
of debating its impact on society at large. It is yet another case of
dissent being barred from public life. Literature criticising capitalism is described by the UK's Department of Education as taking
an 'extreme political stance', rather in the manner of terrorism,
which does not say much for their commitment to free speech.[42]
Presumably 'extreme' is to be understood in such contexts as 'anti-
right-wing'. Authoritarianism creeps up on one incrementally in

just such a fashion as this and it can take over the public sphere if it is not monitored exceedingly carefully.

It would help too if political life was less antagonistic in tone than it presently is, with parties consistently demonising each other to the extent of creating a toxic atmosphere in public life in general. Basic respect for others is often missing from politics, especially when the government in question is on the extreme right of the political spectrum and regarding its opponents as enemies of the state. The longer dissent is treated in that manner, the more the public will assume that it is acceptable for them to hold the same views and to air them when and where they choose. Political leaders like President Trump hardly set much of an example, with his taunts and insults of anyone who disagrees with him; behaviour like that cannot be considered in the spirit of democracy, far less an invitation to engage in dialogue and most certainly not an invitation to express dissent, even by high-profile public officials like the director of the FBI. Dissent calls for a large-scale public campaign to make everyone think about whether they are guilty of such attitudes – and then to examine the reasons why, with a view to changing their social behaviour (and particularly their social media behaviour). Prejudice and bigotry ought to fall on deaf ears and the first stage would be to encourage individuals to work through their beliefs as rigorously as they could, in order to identify where they might be guilty of this themselves. Any of us is capable of making that mistake, of defaulting into bias almost by reflex: the occasional intervention from our 'inner conspiracy theorist' that catches us off guard.

Conclusion: speaking to a future age

Dissent is under sustained attack from various quarters therefore, with the pressure being exerted on it by many governments and organisations growing markedly in recent times, to the point where it constitutes a very significant threat to the practice of democracy. It is a situation in which the limits of democracy are becoming ever more apparent, since it can be, and is being, manipulated by unscrupulous politicians. These politicians are mainly on the right at present, but as the history of communism reveals, the left is more than capable of doing the same when it has the chance; left authoritarianism is no more attractive than right authoritarianism and it is not what is being defended in these pages. Dissent has its work cut out for it in resisting the power of governments, which almost invariably strive to minimise opposition, no matter what their ideological position; yet it needs to be recognised as an absolutely crucial part of the political process, without which it can so easily turn authoritarian and even totalitarian, demolishing the hard-won system of civil liberties and human rights on which liberal democracy so depends. As Steven Levitsky and Daniel Ziblatt have warned us, democracies can 'die' and we cannot take their continued existence for granted, a possible scenario which is beginning to worry many in the US in the aftermath of the 2020 elections, where so many time-honoured conventions about the conduct of politics were comprehensively trashed.[43] Anne Applebaum makes a similar point, noting that '[g]iven the right conditions, any society can turn against democracy', as does Peter Geoghegan, for whom the influx of 'dark money' in electoral campaigns signals an existential threat that the system is ill geared to resist.[44] The case for dissent needs to keep being made, over and over again, therefore, to prevent that situation from ever becoming the norm and governments being able to avoid detailed scrutiny: the ethics of public discourse are at stake in this contest. Many current governments would be only too happy to resort to anti-democratic behaviour to ensure that lack of public scrutiny stayed the case, and while emergency powers may well be necessary when large-scale crises hit nation states, they can be abused to that end – as we are in the painful process of discovering. Neither the political centre nor the left can afford to let trends like this roll on unchecked without offering concerted opposition; controlling the political sphere to that degree can never be condoned. This study amounts to an invitation to dissent in order to ensure that we avoid that fate and the bleak prospect it holds of being propelled into a 'global political winter'. It is not being alarmist to say such things either, merely realistic as current socio-political trends go; that is the message that the Green movement, particularly the radically oriented 'degrowth' campaign that it has generated, continues to broadcast in the face of our obsession with economic growth and the dire effect it is having on the planet ('Green dissent', as I will be describing it, is one of the topics to be covered in the concluding chapter).[45]

The American Supreme Court judge Ruth Bader Ginsburg, who died in 2020, was famed for her principled defence of dissent, regularly excepting herself from the judgments reached by the majority of her far more conservatively minded Supreme Court colleagues. 'Dissents speak to a future age' was her rationale for her position, and we might adapt that as a slogan for this project as 'dissenters speak to a future age':[46] an age, hopefully, where there are still dissenters in operation striving their hardest to keep a global political winter at bay.

Notes

1. Bleiker, *Popular Dissent, Human Agency and Global Politics*, p. 2.
2. Dorfman, 'Refractions: Dissent and Memory', p. 20.
3. Mudde, *The Far Right Today*, pp. 1–2.
4. Mishra, *Bland Fanatics: Liberals, Race and Empire*.
5. See Sarat, *Dissent in Dangerous Times*.
6. See Traverso, *Left-Wing Melancholia*; Rancière, *Disagreement*.
7. See Mouffe, *For a Left Populism*.
8. Diamond, 'Facing Up to the Democratic Recession'.
9. See Leslie, *Conflicted*.
10. See, for example, the various contributions to Wilson and Swyngedouw, *The Post-Political and its Discontents*.
11. Orwell, 'The freedom of the press'.
12. See Certeau, *The Practice of Everyday Life*.
13. Orwell, 'The freedom of the press'.
14. There are numerous studies of the Arab Spring and its aftermath; see, for example, Noueihed and Warren, *The Battle for the Arab Spring*, and Danahar, *The New Middle East*.
15. Bayat, *Life as Politics*, p. 4.
16. Ibid., p. 12.
17. See in particular Arendt, 'Civil Disobedience'.
18. Gessen, *Surviving Autocracy*.
19. Caygill, *On Resistance*, p. 10 (emphasis in original).
20. Falk, 'The History, Paradoxes, and Utility of Dissent', p. 28.
21. Butler, 'Critique, Dissent, Disciplinarity', p. 792.
22. Collins and Skover, *On Dissent*.
23. The research was published in the prestigious medical journal *The Lancet* in 1998, but was based on a very small survey of only twelve cases and

when its findings could not be replicated by a series of other research studies the journal proceeded to retract it. Despite its repudiation by the medical authorities, however, it continues to be cited by anti-vaxxers, who, in true conspiracy theory fashion, regard the official response as a cover-up. The main researcher involved, Dr Andrew Wakefield, is now a campaigner against the Covid vaccine.

24. Sunstein, *Conspiracy Theories and Other Dangerous Ideas*, p. 5.
25. Larson, *Stuck*, p. xvii.
26. Ibid., p. xx.
27. Smith and Wong, 'QAnon. Trump tacitly backs conspiracy movement'.
28. Scorer, 'Save the Children', p. 23.
29. Sunstein, *Conspiracy Theories and Other Dangerous Ideas*, pp. 3, 2–3.
30. Lawton, 'The war against reality'.
31. Fazackerley, 'Academics fear naming and shaming for leftwing views'.
32. See 'About', Turning Point UK website, https://tpointuk.co.uk/about (accessed 28 September 2021).
33. See Professor Watchlist website, https://professorwatchlist.org (accessed 28 September 2021).
34. See 'Education Watch', Turning Point UK website, https://tpointuk.co.uk/education-watch (accessed 28 September 2021).
35. See Turning Point USA website, https://tpusa.com (accessed 28 September 2021).
36. Falk, 'The History, Paradoxes and Utility of Dissent', p. 25.
37. See Honneth, *The Struggle for Recognition*.
38. Smith, *No Platform*, p. 2.
39. Riley, *The Free Speech Wars*.
40. Wendling, *Alt-Right*, p. 9.
41. Jean-François Lyotard has, rather controversially, come up with the term 'the jews' for all such groups; the lower-case initial differentiating them from the Jewish race itself, but indicating that they have suffered similarly from injustice. See Lyotard, *Heidegger and 'the jews'*.
42. Busby, 'English schools told not to use anti-capitalist material'.
43. See Levitsky and Ziblatt, *How Democracies Die*.
44. Applebaum, *Twilight of Democracy*; Geoghegan, *Democracy for Sale*.
45. For degrowth, see Latouche, *Farewell to Growth*.
46. See 'Ruth Bader Ginsburg in pictures and her own words'. For more of Ginsburg on the subject of dissent, see Ginsburg with Hartnett and Williams, *My Own Words*.

Chapter 2

The State and Dissent: The Limits of Democracy

Liberal democracy is in principle designed to prevent the growth of authoritarianism in the political sphere, with governments being subject to the continual scrutiny of opposition parties and regular elections offering voters the option of change if they become dissatisfied with the record of the office-holders. Various extra-governmental checks and balances have been built into the process, such as an independent judiciary and a free press with the licence to hold government to account through an ongoing critique of its policies; it is always a bad sign when a government starts to bully either of these institutions, an indication that it is not respecting the system as it should and may not be worthy of the electorate's trust as guardian of the democratic order. One-party rule, as exists in various countries in the non-Western world, is the supposed antithesis to this model and it has a notoriously poor track record as regards respecting human rights; but a similar effect can be achieved even under a liberal democracy, enabling governments to entrench themselves for substantial periods and to operate in a largely unchecked manner during those. In the 'first past the post' (FPTP) method of electoral politics, it is possible to win a majority large enough to neuter any opposition in a parliament or national assembly – as the Conservative government in the UK currently demonstrates. Critics have called this kind of outcome 'elective dictatorship' to indicate the power it grants for the length of the electoral period, where governments effectively have free rein to curb dissenting voices by passing restrictive legislation (on the media, for example, which is always a convenient whipping boy for a government wanting to demonstrate its power). Such situations reveal the limits of democracy in the way that they reduce the effectiveness of dissent, and they have generated debate on the merits, or otherwise, of alternative systems such as proportional representation (as well as the various forms this can take). Coalition governments, which are more likely to occur under the latter dispensation, cannot afford to be as cavalier as single-party governments elected under FPTP can; if nothing else it is harder to close down dissent from such a position, where all other parties with parliamentary representation have to be considered as at least potential partners (and some strange groupings can come about if circumstances appear to demand them, with parties from opposite ends of the political spectrum sometimes entering into collaboration). It is a more fluid kind of parliamentary system, one in which change can come about more quickly and in which elective dictatorship is extremely unlikely to occur – although forming a government is not as straightforward an exercise and often quite a drawn-out and messy one, which has to be considered a mark against the idea. The extent to which proportional representation might be said to offer greater opportunities for dissent to flourish in a democratic system will be discussed in more detail later in the chapter.

It is also worth speculating whether a federal system might make it easier for dissent to keep authoritarianism in check; that is, as long as it was a federation where real power and autonomy were devolved to each component part. In most existing federal states the central government can still exercise the right of veto and enforce its will on the nation as a whole if it is adamant about the need for a particular piece of legislation to be passed, so this would require a far looser arrangement than in the UK, for example (or even the US to some extent, as will be discussed below). It is not difficult to envisage setting up such a system, however, because most countries have marked differences in both social and political terms between the various regions that make them up. The UK consists of four separate countries, and differences are to be found even within each of them (in England, for example, there is a definite north–south divide to be noted, and London differs enormously from the rest of the country). It is always worth remembering that if we go back to the aftermath of the Roman withdrawal, England consisted of several kingdoms and the regional characteristics of these are still evident even in our own time.

As noted in Chapter 1, it will be a key concern of this study to determine whether it could support all forms of political dissent, since dissent can come from the radical right as much as from left-wing or liberal sources – as we have already seen with the Turning Point movement, as well as the Trump presidency and the Brexit campaign. The radical right is capable of expressing its dissent against the system in racist or misogynist terms, in other words to be dissenting on behalf of prejudice and bigotry, deploying social media to considerable effect to spread its message, as both President Trump and the Brexit campaign did with such depressing success. That will not be the kind of dissent to be defended here, however, where it will be taken to be broadly liberal in character and resolutely anti-authoritarian in its objectives, opposing rather than promoting prejudice and bigotry – which 'dark money' is only too ready to bankroll behind the scenes so as to undermine the system to its own advantage.[1] As also discussed in the previous chapter, conspiracy theory is to be ruled out on the similar ground of being dogmatic rather than truly oppositional; its aims run counter to democratic ideals, since it is plainly not open-minded nor willing to listen to evidence to the contrary (except to define it as fake news). Conspiracy theorists will stick to their position regardless of what happens, supremely confident that only they know what is really going on and that the rest of us are foolishly allowing ourselves to be manipulated by sinister hidden forces skilled at the art of cover-up.

The response of the state to whistleblowing will also be considered in this chapter. Although officially encouraged, it is not always acted upon by the ruling powers, or quite often (conveniently) buried in its bureaucratic system until it loses its urgency and other stories take over the news. In consequence, whistleblowers can find themselves being ostracised, with their career prospects badly damaged as a result of their action (and the odd death threat thrown in for good measure), once again revealing the uneasy relationship between the state and dissent.

The problem of democracy

To warn that democracies can 'die' is to reveal one's support of democracy in general and liberal democracy in particular. I lean towards social democracy myself, but to all intents and purposes that is a subset of the liberal tradition prevailing in the West, so what follows applies to both. By contextualising my argument largely within that political tradition, I am by no means suggesting that it is a perfect model or that it needs no improvement. Before it can be improved, however, it has to overcome the threat posed by the right-wing extremism that has been asserting itself so boldly in the political arena of late, with, as Wendy Brown has so succinctly summed it up, 'its curious combination of libertarianism, moralism, authoritarianism, nationalism, hatred of the state, Christian conservatism, and racism'.[2] Everything in that combination is bent on suppressing dissent and keeping it suppressed, thus exposing democracy's limits again and again. Brown wants us to resist this tide of 'antidemocratic politics' as strongly as we can, but to a theorist like Jacques Rancière the problem lies in the liberal democratic model itself, which in his view compromises dissent before it can even make its points. This can be traced back to the fact that, from the very beginnings of democracy, its politics has been based on a rationalisation of inequality, rendering it 'the sphere of activity of a common that can only ever be contentious'.[3] In order to maintain that structure of inequality democracies need 'policing', which in Rancière's usage equates to something like ideology (although that is not a term he likes): 'The police is thus first an order of bodies that defines the allocation of ways of doing, ways of being, and ways of saying, and sees that those bodies are assigned by name to a particular place and task.'[4] Both democracy and the politics that it generates are based, as he unequivocally puts it, on 'a wrong' that 'cannot be settled'.[5] That is, however, precisely what modern 'consensus democracy' (or 'postdemocracy' as he dubs it) tries to obscure.[6] Rancière's position is that politics should be thought of instead in terms of dissensus, 'a conflictive world' rather than one in which consensus is used to cover up the wrong that perpetuates inequality.[7] As he neatly puts it, in a swipe at Marxism and all totalising theories of politics, 'class war is the actual reality of politics, not its hidden cause'.[8] There can be no 'end of politics', whether in the Marxist or any other sense, and all efforts to claim there is or can be are to be rejected.

For all Rancière's championship of dissensus and the more radical form of democracy that it envisages, it is not all that clear how we could ever escape from the clutches of democracy's policing: 'How some new politics could break the circle of cheerful consensuality and denial of humanity is scarcely foreseeable or decidable right now,' as he pessimistically remarks in the conclusion to his book *Disagreement: Philosophy and Politics* (an instance of 'left melancholia' perhaps).[9] Liberal democracy, with its conspicuous orientation towards consensus, does not seem worth preserving for this theorist, but it could be argued that this is to leave us at the mercy of the radical right, who would be only too happy to take advantage of such an impasse. The fact that the right is so obsessed with suppressing dissent means that it considers dissent an impediment to its plans, so we have to assume that it is worth engaging in. Democracy may be less than perfect, but that is no reason for giving up on it altogether; one might say that it is worth defending, not so much for what it is, as for what it might be. Dissent is a critical part of the process by which such improvement can come about, an expression of what for John Medearis is democracy's innately oppositional character; it is to be regarded as a sign of political vitality.[10]

'Liberal' is another term that poses problems, particularly when it is also the root of 'libertarianism' and 'neoliberalism', terms which can so easily become entangled with it. Both of the latter terms push the notion of freedom further than the average liberal or liberal democrat would wish to do, ideally wanting individuals to be free of any regulation whatsoever on their activities. It is an attitude which suits the right more than the left, given that it is in favour of minimal government intervention in human affairs, believing that the private sector is far superior to the public and should therefore be left to its own devices. Social democracy could not agree with such aims and liberal democracy has its reservations too – although right-oriented governments that come to power in the latter context will tend to test how far they are able go in that direction without alienating their electorate. Their efforts have, as Brown complains, 'intensified the nihilism, fatalism, and rancorous resentment already present in late modern culture' to the general detriment of the Western democratic order, which, as Bonnie Honig has bluntly put it, has been left in a dangerous state of 'disrepair' in consequence.[11] Neoliberalism is anything but liberal as far as traditional liberalism goes; in the words of Thomas Frank, it has led to an 'end of economic democracy'.[12] The same can be said of libertarianism, which has been in the forefront of resistance to government-sponsored vaccination programmes during the pandemic. Even mask-wearing has been treated by libertarians as an assault on their personal liberties – as in the case of President Trump's supporters, who continue to turn up to Republican Party rallies unmasked, despite the advice to the contrary of the nation's health authorities. Anti-authoritarianism in this case puts others' welfare at risk, which is certainly not the role I envisage for it in the political arena. Libertarianism tends towards the selfish and opposition to authority has to have something higher-minded behind it than that – as whistleblowing manifestly does.

Whistleblowing v. authority

In principle, democratic governments are in favour of whistleblowing, in practice, noticeably less so; most such governments regard it as a nuisance at best and usually try to find ways of neutralising its impact (unless of course it reflects badly on their parliamentary opponents and can be used against them). One-party, authoritarian states like China are considerably harsher on whistleblowers, automatically treating them as enemies of the state, vociferously denying the reality of their claims and doing their utmost to prevent their message from reaching the wider public, as notoriously happened in the outbreak of the coronavirus in Wuhan in early

2020, which the Chinese government did its best to cover up in its early stages. As this episode indicates, whistleblowing can be a matter of life and death.

Whistleblowing is a particularly principled form of dissent, given that it places the individual (or group) initiating it in such a difficult position, taking on either a government or a large organisation that has far superior resources to call on to defend itself against any charges made. Organisations invariably close ranks when their integrity is challenged, especially if there is a claim of criminal activity involved – such as putting public safety significantly at risk or misusing public funds. All too often whistleblowers will discover themselves being pushed out of the organisation they work for and having their own integrity called into question, possibly even facing criminal charges brought by their employers as a retaliatory measure – which sends out an unambiguous message to anyone else thinking of making such a move. Organisations are more than capable of fighting dirty in such circumstances and usually will if the stakes are high. The cases of such recent celebrated whistleblowers as the American Edward Snowden indicate how awkward a situation these individuals can discover themselves in once they go public. Snowden is now effectively a refugee in Russia, facing criminal charges if he ever returns to the US. It requires considerable courage to take such a step, which can easily blight your life indefinitely, leaving you socially very isolated. It is easy to see why both governments and companies can get away with dubious, even outright dangerous, practices for years, given the difficult situation that whistleblowers will place themselves in for drawing these to public attention. Clive Ponting, the British civil servant who leaked secret government documents during the Falklands War which he felt deserved to be known to the general public (they related to the controversial sinking of the Argentinian cruiser *General Belgrano*), was prosecuted under the Official Secrets Act despite having confessed to his action and then resigned his post. Although he was subsequently acquitted, his civil service career was over. Ponting's book on the topic was titled *The Right to Know*, which sums up the whistleblowers' creed. Whistleblowing is a classic case of telling those in power what they do not want to hear – and will do their best to prevent being heard by the wider public.

Snowden's experience was far tougher than Ponting's. His inside information concerned the vast surveillance scheme that had been built up by the US's National Security Agency, which was systematically collecting all the public's communications (phone, email, social media exchanges etc.; GCHQ in the UK were doing the same), meaning that almost all our personal details were known to the intelligence community.[13] There is no doubt that this information deserved to be made public, given its political implications. It reveals quite starkly the state's ability to hunt down dissenting voices and stifle opposition if it decides it is in its interests to do so. Surveillance on this scale runs directly counter to democratic ideals, where one's private life is supposed to be protected, and it makes dissent significantly harder to organise or participate in. The American state's response to Snowden indicates just how serious it is about preventing dissent from being able to operate. Intensive surveillance of the population is something we have come to expect from fascist or communist states (as in East Germany's huge force of informants working for the notorious Stasi secret police force), but not from liberal democracies, and it has to be considered a very worrying trend.

The Trump administration's response to an accusation made against it by a whistleblower working within the government set-up itself, which triggered the impeachment charge against the president that was eventually rejected by the Senate in 2020, provides yet another example of just how difficult such a situation can be for the accuser. The complaint was made to an inspector general in the Intelligence Service, only for Trump to demand the complainant's name, which of course would have made that individual's position as a government employee untenable, as well as exposing him or her to online abuse from avid Trump supporters around the country (never slow to spring into action). Since the inspector general in question, Michael Atkinson, refused to divulge the name, Trump fired him, a not very subtle warning to potential whistleblowers anywhere (plus anyone supporting their cause) as to the dangers of daring to take on the rich and powerful.

Malice on the part of the whistleblower is simply assumed by high-ranking figures such as presidents, or organisation heads anywhere, who do not tend to back down or admit liability in such instances; instead, they do their best to undermine the credibility of the accuser, drawing on the extensive network of resources available to them. The result in such high-profile cases is often that the whistleblower ends up being treated as the accused. Although there has to be a robust system of checking and verifying the evidence presented (innocent until proved guilty and all that), the lone whistleblower is invariably thrown on to the defensive as if he or she was a mere troublemaker rather than a concerned citizen acting on behalf of the general public. There is little to be gained from whistleblowing unless it is undertaken for such a reason, but as charges and counter-charges steadily build up, it becomes more and more difficult to know who to believe, which is definitely to the advantage of the accused party or parties. The longer such cases drag on, the less interest the public tend to show in them; many just peter out in time with little in the way of clear resolution. Whistleblowers are by no means always vindicated and you have to be very motivated indeed to put yourself in that position, aware that it all might be for nothing. You certainly cannot count on much in the way of official help if you choose to become a whistleblower, regardless of what governments might claim.

Proportional representation v. 'first past the post'

Whether proportional representation leaves more scope for dissent to make its influence felt than the 'first past the post' electoral system is an issue of some considerable importance for liberal democratic politics and one that has drawn a lot of attention from political commentators in recent years.[14] Proportional representation, as noted above, can take many forms, each with its advocates claiming that it best captures the complexity of the public's political views. There is, for example, the 'alternative vote' method, used in Australia, where voters can express their preferences by placing a number opposite each candidate's name on the ballot paper: 1, 2, 3 and so on, depending on the number of candidates standing for the seat. The 'single transferrable vote' (STV) system also enables voters to express a choice of candidates, with the votes being transferrable to other candidates under certain specified circumstances. Neither system is as straightforward as FPTP in terms of declaring a result in any given constituency and STV in particular can sound very complicated (although it has been successfully in operation in Ireland for most of the republic's history). The renowned election analyst Vernon Bogdanor is a particular advocate of STV, claiming that it would correct the unfairness of FPTP in the UK. His contention is that

> STV allows – indeed encourages – constituents to vote for the kind of representative they want. It is, in this sense, a *transparent* electoral system, one in which the elected representatives tend to reflect the qualities of those who elect them. STV is an electoral system which holds up a mirror to society.[15]

The *Irish Times* agrees with this verdict, calling STV 'one of the most flexible, subtle systems in the world', making a vote in an Irish election 'much fairer' than its equivalent in Britain or America.[16]

There is also the 'two ballot' system, where if no candidate receives at least 50 per cent of the vote on the first ballot, then a second is held, with the number of candidates being whittled down according to the size of their vote (those under a certain percentage being eliminated, although it could also be done by making it a run-off between the top two or three). It is used in the French presidential elections, but could be applicable in parliamentary elections as well, although it would make general elections a longer process, which might not be very popular (one can imagine the complications it would create in a country like America, which already takes several days to declare in presidential elections). It also has to be noted that there is also a greater likelihood of mistakes being made in systems that require multiple counts to be conducted than in FPTP.

Other hybrid systems have been put forward, however, such as 'total representation' (TR), which is presented as 'a simplified variant' of STV.[17] Under this in the UK, constituency MPs would be elected as usual and go to make up 80 per cent of Parliament.

Runner-up candidates would then go into a national pool, which would operate on a proportional representation system to elect the remaining 20 per cent of the Commons' members. Even more radically, the House of Lords would become an elected body, again on TR principles, giving the electorate far greater control over the legislative system than they have at present (reform of the House of Lords has been fruitlessly debated in the UK parliament for over a century now). Leaving aside all the technicalities for the time being, however, the analysis here concentrates on the prospects for dissent under proportional representation systems in general and whether or not these are likely to be better than under FPTP, although it is always worth bearing in mind that, as Bogdanor admits, 'none of the systems of proportional representation yields *exact* proportionality'.[18] Nevertheless, he continues to favour them in general (STV in particular), on the basis that they would lead to different outcomes than FPTP, which is very obviously never going to be as representative of votes cast on a national level.

One of the main arguments against proportional representation is that it makes coalition governments a far more likely outcome, because even small parties might win at least some seats that way, increasing the number of competing ideological positions within the parliamentary framework. Large parties, on the other hand, find it correspondingly more difficult to win outright majorities (although it is always theoretically possible and in some existing cases actually does happen), compelling them to negotiate with other parties in order to build a large enough grouping to form a government. The good side of this is that elective dictatorship is also far less likely to result. Compromise has to play a key role in the negotiations, so other viewpoints are always having to be respected (or at least tolerated) by any large party striving to put together a viable coalition. There is an intrinsically more democratic feel to proportional representation because it far more accurately expresses the views of the electorate than FPTP, where large parties can win parliamentary majorities – and sometimes very significant ones – without an overall majority of the popular vote. This is increasingly the norm in countries like the UK, where percentages in the thirties can be ample enough for an electoral victory. Individual seats can be won with quite a low percentage of the vote too, which has to raise questions about the credibility of the system (the more parties that stand in any given constituency, the lower a percentage that will be required for victory as well). Holders of minority viewpoints are better catered for by the proportional representation system, therefore, knowing that their votes are more likely to count towards representation of some kind, and thus at least a potential route into government, than FPTP can ever offer; proportional representation cannot guarantee that, but it does at least increase the possibility. Again, that seems a more democratic outcome and one that potentially could alter the political landscape of a country like the UK quite significantly.

The Liberal Democrats have campaigned for proportional representation for years, but predictably it has never found much favour with the nation's two largest political parties, who recognise that it would turn the Lib Dems into a major electoral force once again, thus reducing their own power quite considerably. It could also lead to a growth in the number of small parties, which could make coalitions even more likely; although this could be restricted if there was a threshold of the national vote that had to be reached for parties to gain representation to the parliamentary body (as applies in Germany, for example). Whether that is in the democratic spirit is open to debate, but it would probably have the effect of cutting down opportunities for dissent.

The downside of proportional representation is that it usually means extensive negotiations have to be conducted to make a fully functional government possible and that it can encourage a somewhat bland form of consensus politics, with every party in the coalition set-up having to water down their policies to some extent to gain the support of others. Given the often wide range of ideological positions involved in a coalition government, there is a much greater risk of internal disagreements breaking out over policy and the coalition collapsing: compromise has its limits, too. It could be argued, therefore, that for all its bad points the FPTP system generally delivers more stable governments, even if it does not constitute an accurate picture of what the electorate as a whole actually thinks (its easiness to run is a definite factor in its favour too). This stability comes at the expense of smaller parties and minority views, however, and that has to mean that dissent is in a less favourable position to make its effect felt politically than in a system weighted towards coalitions. You have to be in the political mainstream to feel that you have a proper stake in the system, and while that does reduce the impact of extremist views, it can also have the effect of making anything other than a main-stream position look extremist.

Ultimately, as Bogdanor has pointed out, proportional representation is 'an *ideal* or *principle*', concerned to make individual votes count as much as they possibly can, although it is always worth remembering his qualification that what this might mean in practice is looking for the system that 'has the smallest number of defects'.[19] One of the primary defects in the turn to the right we are witnessing at present is the suppression of dissent, so it would be a priority to ensure that this did not appear in that smallest number. Arguably, one way round all such defects is to introduce more referenda into the political process, because that is where full proportionality is achieved for the individual vote. Whether you agree with the result of the Brexit referendum or not (and I do not), it does suggest that referenda could play a useful role in proportional representation as a way of minimising its defects. They can be abused and manipulated (as I think they were with Brexit), but then so can any political system; their proportional-ity, however, seems undeniable, although I concede that they can divide opinion nevertheless. Aharon Nathan, for example, argues that the Scottish and Brexit referenda 'tore into the fabric of our political and social cohesion' and he finds no place for them in TR.[20] Whether there was as much cohesion there as he thinks is, however, another matter.

Rethinking federalism

Federalism exists around the world in various forms, with a greater or lesser degree of central control involved in each instance. It is a concept that can still be tinkered with, however; there is 'no fully fledged theory of federalism' to offer guidance to those so inclined, as Michael Burgess has pointed out, just examples drawn from existing systems, all of them flawed to some extent or other.[21] The point would be to see if it could be loosened significantly enough to achieve a more democratic working mode, especially when it comes to expressing dissent and thus checking the development of authoritarian tendencies in the central government. It is the extent of the devolution of powers that is the critical factor here and that is invariably a point of contention in any federal set-up, as the sample considered below will reveal. In their very useful primer on the subject, Mark J. Rozell and Clyde Wilcox identify three main types of federal arrangement: unitary, confederate and federal. Unitary systems feature strong central control, confederate more regional control, and federal a more complex system where 'overlapping and shared powers generally exist between the national and subnational units, and there are also distinctive areas of authority that belong uniquely to each unit'.[22] The latter describes the system in the US and for all that it appears to offer a high degree of flexibility between central and regional control (not to mention a bewildering range of variations as to how this is applied in the case of each particular state), it is increasingly showing signs of internal strain that create opportunities for, but can also hamper, the cause of dissent.

The EU offers some interesting pointers as to how such a looser federation might be constructed (constituting a confederate system in Rozell and Wilcox's classification), as well as some others indicating what does not work or creates the kind of internal tensions that led to Brexit, which has to be considered a blemish on its record. The support previously expressed by such as Michael Burgess for the further development of federalism within the EU has since been overtaken by events; yet although the Brexiteer community will vehemently reject such a value judgement, the EU has been a success story in many ways as well as a powerful advertisement for the benefits of federalism.[23] Europe has been a much more peaceful place overall since it was founded – no mean feat considering the conflict-ridden European history of the last century or two – and it has established a particularly successful free trade area, which it has to its credit widened substantially since the break-up of the Soviet bloc to include a clutch of eastern

European nations, despite the problems caused by incorporating several much weaker economies into its system. There does seem to be a genuinely idealistic cast to the EU's organisational ethos, a commendable desire to improve the relations between its partners and to widen the opportunities open to their citizens through the policy of free movement around the bloc. Where questions start to arise is over the issue of national sovereignty, which lay right at the heart of the Brexit campaign and referendum. The EU has grown into a very large bureaucracy and that does create worries about the infringement of national sovereignty, which the Brexit campaign made full use of with their constant criticism of 'Brussels' – and it has to be conceded that it resonated very powerfully with the general population, although not always in a very positive way (a particularly jingoistic nationalism was one rather depressing result, in England at least).

The relationship between the European Parliament and national assemblies gives rise to concerns too and again these are easy to exploit for populist gain, with populist politicians accusing EU supporters in their own countries of being unpatriotic. Given that this kind of nationalism is precisely what the EU was designed to counter, it does suggest that something has gone wrong in how the system has developed. It is not just in the UK that aggressive nationalism revealed itself either; anti-EU movements can be found throughout most of the member states, especially its larger countries (both France and Italy are noteworthy in this respect, and the emergence of fascist parties in Germany is a particularly worrying reminder of the past that the EU has sought to distance itself from). National identity is a phenomenon that still has to be taken into account in any confederate-style set-up and for all its efforts the EU has been unable to overcome this entirely – to make being a European citizen a more attractive prospect than being a British one, in a crucial test case. (This seems less of a problem in smaller states, which are more aware of the need to be part of a larger grouping to protect themselves, both politically and economically.) Paradoxically enough, being British should make it easier to juggle several citizenship identities at once: Scottish and British or Welsh and British, for example. Adding European to Scottish and British, as in my own case, does not seem so problematic a move: such identities do not have to clash, they can easily co-exist – a bit like having a federal system inside you, perhaps, with overlapping and shared loyalties.

The EU is in a battle against populism, therefore, and it would seem to be the populists who are on the side of dissent (as it seemed with Brexit too), being able to present themselves as opposing a bureaucracy which is out to keep them in a state of submission. The fact that the EU has become progressively more ambitious in its centralising plans, to the extent of envisaging united armed forces, has played into the hands of the populists, who can accuse it of imperialism; the larger any political organisation becomes the more it leaves itself open to such a charge. That was a fear that the Brexit campaign was able to exploit, claiming that it demonstrated the dangers of federalism and how it could swamp British national identity (fragmented though that already is, as noted above). Even post-Brexit it is a tension within its set-up that the EU has still to resolve and that it may have to face up to again as nationalist movements grow in its member states. Any federal system has to be careful not to overcentralise and it has to be admitted that the EU does invite attack on that score, moving from its early days as a fairly loose confederation based largely on trade into a more politically controlling form of organisation with its own parliament, suggesting it had aspirations to evolve into a unitary system. The parliament has inspired little public support, however, with MEPs being elected on often scandalously low voter turnouts in the UK as a case in point.

In fact the concept of sovereignty is more apparent than real, as no nation state can be in complete control of its destiny in a world system where stock markets and investors have the power to bring down economies if they lose confidence in them, as can happen at any time and with little warning. A run on the currency is always a sobering event for the government of any country and it rather dramatically reveals the limits of sovereignty as well as democracy, often involving humiliating representations for help to the World Bank and the International Monetary Fund. Nevertheless, sovereignty is still capable of evoking a visceral response in the public at national levels. It should be observed that this visceral response can mean, as it does currently in many of the states of eastern

Europe, blatant suppression of political opposition and restriction of civil liberties and human rights, which might make us see the EU in a more positive light as a centralising authority, since it is opposed to such actions and has made repeated representations to the relevant states about them. The EU in this instance constitutes a check – a necessary dissenting one under the circumstances – on the negative side of sovereignty, the intensely inward-looking discriminatory attitude it can so easily default to, especially when populism comes on the scene to whip up nationalist emotions. Again it has to be pointed out that what might look like dissent, component parts of a federation deciding to opt out of some of its regulations, should not count as such as it is motivated by prejudice and bigotry. On this issue at least, the EU is on the right side of dissent, doing what it should do, standing up for liberal values and defending human rights. States like Hungary and Poland are demonstrating a democratically unacceptable form of sovereignty in that respect: how it can be exploited by populists in the name of a very narrow-minded ideology that eschews humanitarian concerns. All the signs are that the relationship between the EU and its eastern European countries is likely to be a source of problems for quite some time yet. While, under its charter, the EU cannot expel member states for not following its rules, it can suspend some of their rights, which might cause such states to consider exiting the system in the manner of Brexit (there was talk of Greece doing so during its debt crisis in the early 2000s, although ultimately it accepted a bailout from the EU on very harsh terms rather than do so).

Whatever one's position on Brexit, it has to be acknowledged that the EU permitted it to happen, exit from the system being catered for in the Treaty of Lisbon (2009) by the now somewhat infamous Article 50. The UK was not kept in the EU against its will; it asked to join back in the 1960s, was eventually accepted as a member after persistent requests (a point the Brexiteers conveniently ignore), then asked to leave in 2016. Article 50 having been activated, the relevant negotiations on the UK's future relationship with the EU (trading, security etc.) were then instituted. At no point did the EU refuse to allow the UK to honour its referendum result. As Brexit made clear, the extent of the EU's power over a defecting state goes no further than its ability to make the subsequent trade negotiations difficult if it so chooses; calling this a war with the EU, as some of the more extreme Brexiteers did, was just nonsense. Any of the member states is free to come to the same decision as the UK did and opt out, proving that the system does respect the concept of national sovereignty; that is the point of Article 50, although obviously it was hoped that no state would ever want to trigger it. Federal systems as a rule are not as generous as this towards disaffected members, the American Civil War demonstrating how extreme the response to secession can be.

The American Civil War had many complicating factors associated with it, so the nation's federalism is still worth scrutinising closely in terms of the relations it assumes between its constituent parts and centre. On the surface it looks like the most advanced federal system in the world; it is, after all, the 'United States' of America, which implies a significant degree of autonomy for each state in the union. States have the right to impose certain taxes of their own (sales tax being a notable one which varies from state to state, as can also be the case in other federal systems such as Canada) and their regulations on trading and environmental matters can differ as well. It is, however, an autonomy which can be overridden by the central government in the person of the president, who has powers at his or her hand such as the Insurrection Act of 1807, enabling the deployment of the armed forces to put down any severe outbreak of civil disorder, even if the state, or states, where it is happening objects to this intervention into its jurisdiction. The Act was invoked by President George Bush during the Watts riots in Los Angeles in 1992, for example, and then threatened by President Trump as a response to the George Floyd riots in 2020. The Civil War also acts as a potent reminder of how opposed the central government is to states that want to go their own way, of course.

One other intriguing aspect of the relationship is that it appears to allow a president to push back problems to the states for action if he or she decides it is politically advantageous to do that (if also decidedly cynical). The coronavirus pandemic provided an instructive example of this when President Trump told states to find their own resources to deal with the situation – protective equipment, extra hospital staff and so on – rather than expecting central government to step in, and then blamed the state governors for any failures that resulted (especially those of the other party, the Democrats). Critics saw this as an abdication of responsibility by the central government, although it seems consistent with the American federal system and the, supposed anyway, autonomy of the individual states. More problematically, however, it also indicates an unreasonable, and clearly undemocratic, concentration of power in the person of the president if he or she alone is able to rule on the extent and the details of states' autonomy. Autonomy becomes a political football under those circumstances and federalism more than somewhat notional. As interpreted by President Trump at least, federalism is more of an advantage to the central government than it is for any particular state, and it has to be seen as a definite weakness of the system that it is open to such one-sided manipulation, as commentators are beginning to complain.[24] Federalism should include an element of give and take, but this is unmistakably weighted towards the centre, always a problem with such a system.

China's 'one country, two systems' arrangement for the relationship between Hong Kong and the Chinese state also has a federal appearance to it, although once again what it has demonstrated since its implementation in 1997 is the limits of federalism and just how unequal a relationship it can be. Hong Kong has increasingly come under the control of the central government, which has been unwilling to see the two systems diverge to the point where Hong Kong becomes more democratic than the Chinese state deems acceptable to its ideology. Hong Kong's apparent semi-autonomy has been no match for an angry central government backed up by the massive military forces that a nation with a population of over a billion can muster. Any hint of federalism disappears at that point, with little if any evidence of give and take to be noted on the part of the ruling Communist Party. Hong Kong has been given a harsh lesson from the centre as to the, very restricted, limits of its regional power, leaving its future very uncertain.

The UK has a federal system of sorts (rather ad hoc, it would have to be said), although the Westminster Parliament has the power to override decisions taken in the Scottish and Northern Irish parliaments and the Welsh Assembly, if it feels they threaten its own policies. Even so, there is what amounts to semi-autonomy in the other three nations in the Union, with some room for manoeuvre allowed by the system (Scotland and Wales chose to adopt different lockdown policies than Westminster, for example, despite the latter's apparently state-wide instructions). There is no formal system for withdrawing from the Union, although Westminster can consider whether to grant a referendum on that issue if so requested. The Scottish Parliament made that request and a referendum was accordingly held in 2014, in which Scotland decided to stay in the Union. There has been talk of another one since (Brexit having brought it to the forefront of Scottish politics, since the Remain side won the vote there by a significant margin), but Westminster is under no obligation to allow it to go ahead and makes this clear whenever the issue comes up. In that sense it is a less free union than applies in the EU, where exit only requires a formal request from the member state to set the procedure going – as occurred in Brexit. The EU may try to persuade the exiting member to change its mind, as it did with the UK, but it cannot compel it to do so nor refuse to grant the request. The fact that the Westminster Parliament can even turn down a request for a referendum from one of its constituent nations, if it so chooses, signals a very significant gap between two systems which otherwise seem quite similar. There is no UK equivalent of Article 50 to appeal to and the central government is under no obligation to provide one.

No federal system will suit absolutely everyone (just as no proportional representation electoral system will either), so it is a case of identifying the best features of the existing ones and trying to incorporate them into a new model that could claim the largest possible majority support – while also leaving space for dissent to make its voice heard. I would argue that the most critical issue has to be withdrawal from the system and whether provision is made for this in the treaty of union. That need not make a federal system weaker, since all the parties involved know that there is a route out if they do not like the way the union is developing and that they are not trapped indefinitely. The latter is a situation which is all but bound to generate political tensions: the break-up of Yugoslavia into a tangle of small nations still disputing borders with each other decades later is an object lesson here. Federal systems that include an exit strategy – a divorce clause, in effect – seem more democratic than those that do not, which is a mark in the EU's favour. Dissent is being neither suppressed nor marginalised in this case, which is always a healthier condition for any political organisation to be in than being authoritarian. There are few existing federal systems, however, which manage to avoid that latter state altogether; sadly enough, power-hungry, ruthlessly ambitious leaders can emerge in any political set-up you care to name.

What federalism would be wise to avoid, however, is the American Senate system, which leads to a drastic imbalance in terms of what votes are worth, per head of population, that is far worse than either FPTP or any of the forms of proportional representation currently available. All bills that are passed in the House of Representatives, a body elected much in the manner of the UK's House of Commons, then have to pass through the Senate before they go to the president for final ratification, and the Senate is one of the least representative governmental bodies in the world, as each state has two senators regardless of its population. The 2019 figures list Wyoming as the least populated state at 578,000 and California the most populous at over 38 million; yet each has an equal vote on the bills that are put before the Senate. This gives low-population states a hugely disproportionate power when it comes to passing legislation, which becomes particularly problematic when the Senate, as during Trump's presidency, has a majority for one party (the Republicans) and the House of Representatives for another (the Democrats). It does not really matter which way round this is, it cannot be considered democratic as the concept is usually understood; it is loaded in favour of the Senate, giving it the ability to act as a veto on the House's deliberations, which is hardly in the spirit of dissent as I am using the term and more in the nature of a system malfunction. Separation of powers here effectively equals stalemate. The Senate also has the power of veto over cabinet appointments in a new administration, which creates obvious problems if it is controlled by a different party than the presidency. In such cases the power imbalance in the make-up of the Senate once again comes into play, with low-population states such as Wyoming having an equal say to states such as California.

One party can of course control the Senate, the House and the presidency also, as ultimately happened when Trump was defeated (if with the tightest of margins, requiring the vice-president's casting vote to achieve a Democrat majority in the Senate); but the system should not have to depend on that outcome, which obviously can never be guaranteed. Add in the president's power to issue executive orders, which require no approval from either the Senate or the House (a favoured tactic of President Trump, who reportedly made use of it 191 times up to the 2020 election date), and the American system, for all the undoubted idealism that went into its creation, can appear deeply flawed from a twenty-first century democratic perspective, being thrown out of kilter by the role and power of the Senate. The fact that the bicameral legislature system of assembly plus senate is replicated in the individual states themselves (with the exception of Nebraska), with a governor above that in a presidential-style role, indicates that it is firmly embedded in the nation's governance – meaning that the problems just discussed above have to be considered endemic to it. Separation of powers does not always have the effect desired by the nation's founders – a point for all federal systems to bear in mind, especially if they are considering any structural changes to make themselves more responsive to the social and political differences between the various parts of their federation. Relying on constitutional history does not always yield a fair result as far as the expectations of twenty-first-century democracy go. In such cases tradition is acting as a drag on the system, blocking the changes that are necessary to correct unmistakable electoral unfairness. Basically, it is an equal rights issue that is coming to light here and no modern democracy, federal or otherwise, should allow it to go unaddressed.

The Electoral College presents yet another case where small or low-population states have the system weighted towards them by the American style of federalism. It is a fairly arcane system, whereby each state appoints a list of electors, who then cast their vote for the president in the College after the actual election has been completed and the popular votes counted, the original idea behind it being to protect individual states' rights. Since the electors themselves are now chosen by the main political parties (originally the idea was to draw them from prominent local figures, which sounds very open to abuse), that makes voting in the College partisan, although there is also the proviso, mentioned during the 2020 presidential election, that state legislatures could theoretically go against the electoral result and appoint electors for the losing party in that state. That may never happen, of course, but the fact that it is even possible ought to give one doubts about the American electoral system, and it has to remain a worryingly grey area that could well be exploited by the unscrupulous (a permanent presence in political life). Again, as with the Senate, the Electoral College is not apportioned by population (although the discrepancy is not quite so stark as with the latter), with low-population states having a larger list of electors than they should on a purely headcount basis, giving them a greater say in the ultimate decision of the College. The number of electors equals the total of members of the House of Representatives each state has plus its two senators – the latter clearly benefitting states such as Wyoming. Presidential candidates have to win states in order to win the vote in the College, which means that a candidate can lose the popular vote, as Donald Trump did in 2016 by the not insubstantial figure of around three million, yet still be elected president because of the imbalance of power enjoyed by the low-population states – plus the FPTP system involved in having to win individual states to gain their electors. This is a kind of federalism that is in desperate need of rethinking, because if anything would seem to justify a decision by popular vote it would be a presidential election, in the style of a referendum if you like, and any system which cannot provide that is surely ripe for restructuring. The American system as it is currently constituted is not really set up for that kind of process, however, as those who benefit from power imbalances do not give them up lightly. Federalism will continue to be under strain in America as long as this situation is allowed to continue; yet again, the principle of equal rights is being violated.

Perhaps the US system is in fact less than an ideal model for federalism anywhere and more of a warning as to how it can go wrong in terms of respecting the will of the majority. Even the best of intentions cannot always deliver fairness in this area and elective dictatorship exercised by a minority, as can happen with the Senate, is never a good advertisement for democracy. Rozell and Wilcox have summed up the dilemma this presents as follows: 'Are current problems in American democracy the result of a flawed system? Americans are not accustomed to asking that question.'[25] After the turbulence of the Trump presidency years, however, it is one that they ought to be considering very seriously indeed. The 2020 election revealed the weaknesses of the American constitutional set-up in stark detail and if the system nevertheless held together (just), that may not always be the case. It now looks distinctly vulnerable; as David Runciman has pithily put it, '[i]f Trump is the answer, we are no longer asking the right question'.[26] If nothing else, the far right now knows how to spread doubt about the electoral system and that does not go away so easily, especially in a country with such a propensity towards belief in conspiracy theories (QAnon is making significant inroads into the Republican Party in the aftermath of Trump's defeat, a phenomenon that will need careful monitoring). The storming of the Capitol building by a pro-Trump mob in an attempt to disrupt Congressional certification of the Electoral College results in January 2021 offers a warning as to where that doubt can lead, raising fears for the future. When mob action of this kind erupts (an attempted coup as many commentators saw it, if, thankfully, not a very organised one), that is an example of dissent gone very wrong; a natural culmination of what Masha Gessen regards as Trump's 'declaration of war against the American system of government as currently constituted'.[27] While street protests can be defended on dissent grounds (as in Belarus and, more recently, Myanmar), a mob breaking into government buildings because it lost an election most certainly cannot; that is the tactics of fascism and where the failure to ask the right questions leads.

Just to be provocative, one of those questions might be whether a presidential system is suited to democracy at all. As long as it is a largely ceremonial role, as it is in many other countries, then it poses no particular problems, but when it grants political power on the American scale then it runs the very real risk of developing into authoritarian rule. It may have been avoided this time around in the US, but the weaknesses of the system have been shown up very ominously by the Trump regime and who is to say they will not be taken advantage of by some future president (with Trump's return a not impossible scenario)?

Globalisation and dissent

Globalisation also reveals the limits of democracy and how dissent can be marginalised within that system when economics is allowed to dictate the political agenda – as it invariably will under neoliberalism. The citizens of Western liberal democracies have benefitted from the lower prices for many manufactured goods that have come about because of the outsourcing of production to the developing world, with its far lower production costs. That is one of globalisation's great selling points and it has promoted it relentlessly: savings passed on to you the consumer, and so on. The downside is that many jobs have been lost in the West as a result of so much of its production being transferred to cheaper labour markets (globalisation is something else that undermines sovereignty quite easily). There have been dissenting voices over the resultant job losses, but as it is the corporate sector that has chosen to go down this route, since it increases its profits, governments are limited as to what they can do. Moving your production to the developing world also has the advantage for this sector of not having to deal with trade unions (or at best, fairly weak ones by Western standards, easily controlled by their government), meaning that strike action for higher wages or better working conditions is far less likely to occur; that too pushes up profits and is a win–win situation for multinationals. At its best, trade unionism acted as a check on capitalism, a form of opposition within a *laissez-faire* economic system with a distinctly anti-social side with respect to worker welfare: economic dissent, as it were (although it has to be noted that it has been in sharp decline throughout the West for several decades now). There is the further problem that multinational corporations are extremely difficult to regulate as many of them are registered in tax havens, where national governments are not supposed to intervene. Dissent over that system is certainly well justified, although it struggles to be all that effective, despite periodic outcries over damaging revelations about dealings there, as happened with the notorious Panama Papers (which named several prominent international political figures amongst those who were benefitting).[28] For all that they might want the multi-nationals to pay more in the way of taxes, and at present what the larger ones pay is quite paltry, most Western governments are staunch supporters of capitalism and generally reluctant to restrict its operations to any really significant degree. The socialist model of economics has more or less disappeared from the contemporary political scene, with even China having abandoned it in favour of a state-controlled capitalism that is firmly integrated into the global economy. Tax havens mark a fault line in democracy, where economic factors are bringing out the extent to which they have become the dominant force in policy-making.

Amongst the dissenting voices to the neoliberal economic regime that globalisation has fostered have been economic theorists such as Thomas Piketty, who argues forcefully for a far more regulated, as well as more heavily taxed, private sector, in order to address the economic inequalities currently being felt around the globe, inequalities which really ought to raise questions about the claims made for the globalisation model. Piketty notes a 'resurgence of inequality after 1980 [that] is due largely to the political shifts of the past several decades, especially in regard to taxation and finance', and neoliberalism and globalisation have been major forces behind those shifts (tax havens have also done their not insubstantial bit).[29] Globalisation, however, is too much to the benefit of the corporate sector for it to pay much attention to the political problems that come in its wake. In fact, the only thing which has slowed up globalisation in recent years has been the coronavirus pandemic. How much, if any, longer-term damage to the globalisation project this event might cause is still to be decided (we are still within the grip of the pandemic as I write); but it seems unlikely that the corporate sector would not try to resurrect full-scale globalisation as soon as it became at all feasible, as it is patently in their interest to do so, especially in the aftermath of the economic recession that the pandemic unleashed.

The pandemic has also exacerbated the democratic recession referred to in Chapter 1, but that is of minimal interest to the corporate sector compared to the effect of an economic one.

Another dissenting voice was that of Donald Trump, who promised in his presidential election campaign in 2016 to work to restore the job losses that had occurred in America as a direct effect of globalisation and outsourced production (which had left many previously thriving manufacturing centres like Detroit little more than ghost towns). It was a tactic which gained Trump a lot of popular support, as well as votes, particularly in America's economically depressed 'rust belt' where job losses had been highest, but unlike Piketty this was not an attack on capitalism as a system, just a rather crude method of ensuring that no-one else shared in America's economic success. Trump was dissenting in favour of a particularly narrow form of nationalism (symbolised by his 'Make America Great Again' campaign slogan), behind which lay some deeply regressive ideas on white supremacism, and that does not qualify as dissent as I am defining it. Dissent has to be more principled than that: opposing prejudiced theories and movements such as white supremacism, not endorsing them and the bigotry that goes along with their public expression. The promotion of racist attitudes is to be considered the antithesis of what dissent ought to be about and will be discussed in more detail below.

Trump's constant belittling of the press hardly denotes someone who accepts the importance of a free press to the democratic process either, even though that has been a jealously guarded tradition in the country's history. As well as all that, Trump turned out to be one of the most authoritarian presidents in American history (as evidenced in his frequent recourse to executive orders, bypassing the legislature), thus not much of an advertisement for dissent, especially when you take into account his cavalier treatment of so much of the mainstream media as purveyors of 'fake news' – an accusation he repeated *ad nauseam* (up to and including coverage of the 2020 election results, even from his favoured network, Fox News). Criticism or opposition of any kind is anathema to such a personality, prompting the roll-out of a raft of 'alternative facts' to discredit such activities. We might describe Trump's political creed as 'fake dissent' and indeed, that would be a good way to refer to far-right dissent in general: it is not designed to correct injustice but to mislead and it does so more effectively than is healthy for democracy. Trump's notorious reaction to the 2020 election results took fake dissent to new heights – or should one say depths? – when he refused to accept that he had lost, claiming that voter fraud (rarely an issue of much note in liberal democracies) had been perpetrated on behalf of his opponent on such a vast scale that the election had been stolen rather than won. Dissenting against his nation's electoral system without credible evidence to back up that position (any at all in real terms, hence the abject failure of the various lawsuits the Trump camp filed in state courts) has to stand as a classic example of fake dissent. One suspects as well that the American right will return to this tactic in the future whenever they lose an election at any level. A pessimistic assessment would be that they may well use it as a model and that would not bode well either for America or for liberal democracy in general. Conspiracy theory applied to election results will certainly find supporters – conspiracy always seems to – but it also has the capacity to render a country ungovernable when it undermines the trust in the system of a significant portion of the electorate. If elections turn into a spate of recounts, as the 2020 presidential election did to a certain extent, just because the far right cannot accept defeat, then that will further erode faith in the system and could well project any country into a condition of ungovernability.

Race and the limits of democracy

Few issues show the limits of democracy more clearly than that of race, which continues to bedevil Western societies, most obviously the US in terms of the tense relations between its black and white population (tenser by the day, as I write), but in some form or other most European countries as well. Dealing with racism is to be considered one of the great failings of the democratic system, in that no matter what laws are passed it continues to flourish amongst the general public – even if only in casual asides or social snubs. Discrimination is simply a fact of life for non-whites and it takes events such as the death of George Floyd at the hands of the police for this to break through into the wider public consciousness. The anti-racist protests this incident generated both inside and outside America are an embarrassment to the liberal democratic system, although whether they will alter it for the better remains to be seen: apparent 'watershed' moments of this kind have come and gone in the past. For all the promises that can be made by officialdom as to outlawing it, racism can still express itself in subtle and informal ways that reveal disturbing levels of hypocrisy in both public and private life (the 'unconscious bias' outlined by Pragya Agarwal in her book *Sway: Unravelling Unconscious Bias*), and that has to render it a prime target for dissent, one that both the centre and the left can unite around. Inevitably, the protests have drawn the ire of the right, which can always be relied upon on to treat these phenomena as an issue of law and order rather than social justice and will do its best to deny they have any validity, 'the work of troublemakers' rather than legitimate dissenters being a fairly common, by now extremely cliched, response. The fault lines in democracy become very evident at such points; the public demonstration of dissent triggers officialdom's reflex response to suppress opposition whenever it arises and for whatever reason. Right-wing marches and demonstrations, on the other hand, tend to draw less criticism from authoritarian governments and are often treated far more leniently in terms of charges made.

The George Floyd-inspired anti-racist protests have spread worldwide, however, constituting an excellent example of how Jean-François Lyotard's concept of the 'little narrative' works and how it can maximise the impact of dissent.[30] Dismantling racism is the objective and it cuts across political lines as a cause to rally round despite any ideological differences that may exist amongst the participants. That is the great virtue of the little-narrative model for Lyotard, who regards it as a vehicle for targeted protest directed at specific abuses of power, with no longer-term plans than their correction. In doing so, it provides a model of how to organise dissent so that it does not take on authoritarian traits itself, as can happen with any campaign; dissenters should always be on the lookout for such a development, which can undermine their efforts. It is no accident that governments of the far right are so quick to ban public protests once they attain office (it happened again in the Myanmar army coup of early 2021), recognising the threat they pose to the image they want to project of being in total control of their nation, of representing its only true spirit – with a dose of nationalism generally thrown in for good measure. What others would regard as a democratic right they regard as an act of contempt and they opt for suppression rather than negotiation, considering the latter to amount to an admission of weakness on their part. Hence the heavy-handed tactics that the police, and if necessary the military, are allowed – in fact often openly encouraged – to use under such governments to disperse protestors; the scenes in Portland, Oregon in the summer of 2020 supply ample evidence of this policy in action. Fascist regimes like public spectacles, but only if they are in charge of them, as the Nazis demonstrated with their meticulously choreographed rallies of a decidedly militaristic character; civil disobedience is another matter altogether and will generally draw a disproportionately harsh response.

Dissent and the military

The limits of democracy also come sharply into focus in the armed forces. Military discipline dictates that orders from one's superiors are to be obeyed, not questioned or treated as a subject for debate. This is especially so in wartime, or any armed conflict at all, but it is maintained in peacetime to ensure that the process is habitual. In such a severely hierarchical organisation as the military it is always perfectly clear where power lies and what the individual's duties are; dissent is not tolerated and will be punished if it is ever publicly expressed, say in the refusal to obey an order from a superior. This is the antithesis to the democratic system, which is based on the principle that there are always alternative viewpoints on any political issue and that space has to be made for these to be aired and if possible debated in a rational manner. A decision might even be altered after that occurs. Opposition is a respected position within the democratic realm, but not within its armed forces, so there is a contradiction to be noted: dissent is assumed to be valid everywhere within a democracy, except within one key section of the polity. If dissent is suppressed in a democracy, those behind the action can be challenged; but no such option exists in the military world and anyone entering the armed forces knows that they will be ceding some of their democratic rights once in uniform. The military is a world with different rules in that respect, and it acknowledges no place for scepticism in the ranks; authoritarianism is the norm and it demands obedience. The political establishment depends on this arrangement, because a state where the rank and file military refuse to do as commanded is usually one that is ripe for revolution (as in Russia in 1917). When the army turns against the government, a state is in real trouble.

An obvious problem arises when such a system is in place: what if following orders results in the commission of a war crime? It was not considered defence enough in the trials of Nazis after the Second World War that they were 'just obeying orders', as military personnel everywhere are required to do. In the case of the Nazi regime, refusal to obey would almost undoubtedly have led to the individual's death: fascists are quite ruthless in those situations and do not allow for such liberal niceties as conscience. Disobeying orders if serving in the military forces of a liberal democracy might not lead to one's death, but a court martial would be very likely, especially if the incident occurred during an episode of armed conflict. Democracy sets limits on conscience therefore, which becomes very problematic if conscience fears a war crime is a distinct possibility – and war crimes can be committed even by liberal democracies, as the My Lai massacre, perpetrated by American soldiers during the Vietnam War, demonstrates only too graphically. Liberal democracies, however, tend to deny that they are capable of such things, which merely suppresses the issue concerning the clash between law and conscience that such events inevitably generate. Whistleblowing can become extremely complicated under these circumstances (democratic governments invariably being wary of alienating their military), although it is often the way that such incidents come to light.

It is possible in a liberal democracy to become a conscientious objector during a war, although it requires considerable resolve to go through the process and makes such individuals distinctly unpopular with their fellow citizens, who tend to brand it as cowardice (nevertheless, it is an option that is unlikely to be there in totalitarian states). Whether in a liberal democracy or not, however, the armed forces do not regard dissent as part of their operational model and will do all they can to avoid it ever becoming so. Dissent and military discipline are natural enemies, a situation which can spill over into the political realm if the head of state has a military background; with a few exceptions, such individuals (often in power because of a military coup) regard their word as law and have little patience with political opposition. We only have to think of such examples as General Franco in Spain or General Pinochet in Chile to see how this mind-set can distort the political system in a defiantly anti-democratic fashion, to the significant detriment of dissent. It is worrying, too, that some democratic leaders seem to get on so well with figures like this (yet again a distinction of President Trump), clearly envious of the power they are able to wield over their citizens. We can probably expect more of that if the turn to the far right continues.

Conclusion: the state v. dissent

Put bluntly, no state, whatever its political orientation, much likes dissent, as it calls the government's competence and integrity into question (as well as making plain its deviousness in notorious cases like Edward Snowden's whistleblowing). Politicians in general are notoriously resistant to admitting mistakes or failings on their part and most governments will automatically close ranks against any such charges, denying them or trying to shift the blame for what they are being accused of elsewhere – sadly, an only too typical response which never shows politics in a very good light. The blaming of care homes for the much higher than average death rate occurring there during the Covid pandemic has to be a low point for the current UK government in that regard (although blaming the general public for the higher infection rate that followed the appearance of a variant to the virus at a later point did not reflect particularly well on it either). Few things reveal the limits of democracy more clearly than the treatment accorded to dissent by the ruling powers; if there are any latent authoritarian tendencies in the government's leaders, a not unusual occurrence, then they will come to the surface at such points and dissenters will know what they need to go into action against on the public's behalf. They will also know just how very difficult the government is likely to make it for their dissent to be expressed – as happens with public protests in general, whether against institutionalised racism, G7 or environmental abuse (I will be discussing the latter topic in the context of the role of dissent in the sciences in Chapter 5).

Notes

1. See Geoghegan, *Democracy for Sale.*
2. Brown, *In the Ruins of Neoliberalism*, p. 2.
3. Rancière, *Disagreement*, p. 14.
4. Ibid., p. 29.
5. Ibid., p. 39.
6. Ibid., pp. 95, 101.
7. Rancière, 'The Thinking of Dissensus', p. 7. For a more detailed discussion of the issue, see Rancière, *Dissensus.*
8. Rancière, 'The Thinking of Dissensus', p. 1.
9. Rancière, *Disagreement*, pp. 139–40.
10. See Medearis, *Why Democracy Is Oppositional.*
11. Brown, *In the Ruins of Neoliberalism*, p. 16; Honig, *Public Things.*
12. See Frank, *One Market under God.*
13. Snowden's story has been covered in various books, the most recent of which is by one of the investigative journalists involved in breaking the story. See Gellman, *Dark Mirror.*
14. For a basic introduction to the topic, see Bogdanor, *What Is Proportional Representation?*. The mathematical complexities of actually applying proportional representation (in this case for the EU Parliament and the German Bundestag) are discussed in Pukelsheim, *Proportional Representation.*
15. Bogdanor, *What Is Proportional Representation?*, p. 106 (emphasis in original).
16. Collins, 'Ireland's voting system'.
17. Nathan, *A Pocket Guide to Total Representation (TR)*, p. 7.
18. Bogdanor, *What Is Proportional Representation?*, p. 6.
19. Ibid., pp. 46, 29 (emphasis in original).

20. Nathan, *A Pocket Guide to Total Representation (TR)*, p. 3.
21. Burgess, *Comparative Federalism*.
22. Rozell and Wilcox, *Federalism*, p. xxi.
23. See Burgess, *Federalism and the European Union*.
24. For an analysis of the strain the Trump presidency put American federalism under, as well as the threat posed to American democracy itself, see Thompson et al., *Trump, the Administrative Presidency, and Federalism*.
25. Rozell and Wilcox, *Federalism*, p. 116.
26. Runciman, *How Democracy Ends*, p. 1.
27. Gessen, *Surviving Autocracy*.
28. See, for example, Zucman, *The Hidden Wealth of Nations*. The author pulls no punches about what tax havens are designed to do: 'they all steal the revenue of foreign nations' (p. 1). The sums involved are enormous too, running into many billions of pounds per annum for developed economies, which go to corporate executives in bonuses (often obscenely large) and to shareholders rather than to the public purse.
29. Piketty, *Capital in the Twenty-First Century*, p. 20.
30 For the 'little narrative', see Lyotard, *The Postmodern Condition*. I discuss Lyotard's political theories in detail in Sim, *Lyotard and Politics*.

Chapter 3

The Philosophy of Dissent

Scepticism represents a permanently dissenting voice within philosophical history, casting doubt on the subject's founding principles and thus its ability to construct logical arguments. It can be considered a particularly pure form of dissent, therefore, taking issue with the whole of the philosophical enterprise, or at the very least suggesting that it can never really live up to its claims, which is why it is playing such a central role in this study. One of the main reasons that such a voice is necessary is that Western philosophy has had a distinct tendency towards system-building over the years, as in the work of such figures as Hegel and Marx, the latter having a hugely significant impact on the development of twentieth-century politics in the form of the communist movement. Earlier examples of this approach can be found in the work of religious philosophers in the Christian tradition, whose goal had been to reinforce their theological belief system rather than point out its shortcomings and contradictions, which to a non-believer are all too obvious (the need for divine intervention and miracles to make the system hang together, for example). Gaps were to be glossed over, not emphasised, and the sanctity of the system was to be preserved at all costs. No-one wanted to make the existence of God seem in any way doubtful, or to raise unanswerable objections to any core Christian doctrine. Faith had to win out, and that meant it was the role of philosophy to provide arguments proving the truth of Christian belief. Equally, no communist philosopher would set out to undermine the Marxist world-view or the canon of works lying behind it. The system dictated what could and could not be said and policed all of that very closely indeed, determined to present an image of being in complete control of its area of discourse. From such a perspective dissent of any kind whatsoever could only be viewed as malicious in intent.

Scepticism is critical of all such schemes, arguing that their foundations are unreliable since they depend on unsubstantiated assumptions, and that truth is a relative concept instead of an absolute: certainty, for the sceptic, always remains out of reach – a message that few politicians heed. It is just such an outlook that lies behind much of continental philosophy, notably poststructuralism and postmodernism, both of which espouse relativism and take issue with the idea that meaning can ever be pinned down with exactitude; as Jean-François Lyotard put it, '[w]e are always within opinion' when it comes to discourse and that is especially the case with politics, even if few politicians would ever admit it (nor theologians either).[1] Lyotard also insists that 'it is high time that philosophers abandon the hope of producing a unitary theory as the last word on things. There is no *archè*, nor does the Good exist as a unitary horizon.'[2] In other words, universal theories are a myth and not what philosophy should be concerning itself with. The point of such thinking is to challenge the assumptions that traditional philosophical discourse makes and to prevent it from turning into an orthodoxy. Post-Marxism has performed a similar service in relation to the Marxist tradition of thought, which by the later twentieth century had become very dogmatic and highly resistant to either internal or external critique of its theories and methods. Without internal dissent in particular, political theories and ideologies can become very closed and prone to stagnate, as communism very notably did over the course of the twentieth century until the Soviet system collapsed in the 1980s and 1990s. Ideologues, whether on the right or on the left, do not like their pronouncements being called into question, nor their utter faith in their beliefs; the more that happens the less powerful they appear, and ideologues are obsessed with how they are perceived on that score.

Keeping that kind of dissent alive is the task scepticism sets itself and I would argue that it is socially and politically necessary that it go on doing so as vigorously as it can. The assumption of the certainty of one's beliefs has caused untold misery and damage throughout human history, being taken to justify the actions of many an ideologue and dictator. For the latter character type it can justify anything from brutal colonisation to ethnic cleansing to genocide; doubt must never creep into anything they do or order to be done. Scepticism is the antidote to such thinking and it has a critical role to play in liberal democracies in consequence; it is a means of keeping ideological extremism and demagogic impulses at bay.

I should make it clear before proceeding any further that I do not intend to conduct an in-depth analysis of Marxism here, or of the various critiques of the theory that have come from within its ranks down the years (and Marxism has had its share of these, mainly from outside the Soviet orbit, hence the term 'Western Marxism' to cover a wide range of theorists, from the early work of Georg Lukács through Antonio Gramsci to the rise of post-Marxism in the later twentieth century).[3] There is a massive literature on this subject which continues to grow and features a great deal of infighting that is of interest mainly to insiders rather than the general public – especially since communism has long since ceased to be a factor of any great import in Western political life.[4] As will quickly become apparent below, my own sympathies lie with the post-Marxists, but the debate between them and classical Marxists will be considered in this chapter purely as an example of how dissent comes to be demonised by a totalising ideological vision. It is what Marxism versus post-Marxism reveals in terms of dissent that I will be concerned with, rather than the validity, or otherwise, of key Marxist doctrines.

Philosophy as system-building

The system-building tendency in philosophical history, the drive towards constructing a unitary theory covering all aspects of our existence and mapping out our future, can be seen at its most ambitious in Hegel's *Philosophy of History*, which conceives of human history as the site of the World Spirit's journey to self-realisation:

> Philosophy concerns itself only with the glory of the Idea mirroring itself in the History of the World. Philosophy escapes from the weary strife of passions that agitate the surface of society into the calm region of contemplation; that which interests it is the recognition of the process of development which the Idea has passed through in realizing itself – i.e. the Idea of Freedom, whose reality is the consciousness of Freedom and nothing short of it.[5]

For all the notorious complexity of Hegel's thought, the basic idea is easy enough to grasp: there is a force working through history that carries humanity with it on a journey to its assumed ideal state. Monotheisms assume a similar process, the overall notion being that there is an underlying reason for everything that happens in human affairs and that we are part of that grand plan devised by our particular divine being. The idea is a seductive one, giving a point and meaning to all human existence and turning 'the weary strife of passions' into something far grander. It is an optimistic theory, providing a cure for fatalism and pessimism, so its appeal is understandable: a happy ending awaits humanity – eventually anyway.

History falls into a series of distinct stages in Hegel's theory, with a dominant cultural form giving rise to its antithesis, leading to a new synthesis which in its turn generates yet another antithesis – up to the point where the World Spirit finally achieves the apex of its development in the modern age and the process is complete. Accept its basic premise and a unitary theory unfolds in a rigorously logical manner. Everything that happens in human history can be explained by this scheme, which is all-encompassing in its scope; it is to be understood as a progression to a determinate end, tracing how social existence has evolved on the largest possible scale. (It is an interesting footnote to philosophical history to observe that when Hegel was expounding his ideas in a lecture series at the University of Berlin, Arthur Schopenhauer was outlining his philosophy of pessimism in a competing lecture series, insisting on the ultimate pointlessness of all human efforts.[6]

The differences regarding the course of human history could hardly be more striking: in Hegel everything will end well, in Schopenhauer it can only ever end badly: 'We shall do best to think of life . . . as a process of disillusionment: since this is, clearly enough, what everything that happens to us is calculated to produce.'[7] Hegel's optimistic vision was to draw in far more students to his lectures than Schopenhauer's notably darker version did, although the latter can often seem more prophetic about how human affairs actually work out than the former. Disillusionment is an emotion I suspect most of us are all too familiar with, especially when living through times of burgeoning right-wing extremism and authoritarian politics, not to mention a pandemic that is wreaking havoc around the globe. History since Hegel hardly suggests that we have reached the ideal state of societal development either, not with the many wars that have broken out since, particularly the massively destructive two world wars of the twentieth century.)

Hegel's teleological conception was later to be reworked by Marx and Engels into a prototype for world revolution in *The Communist Manifesto*, again envisaging human history as a series of determinable stages progressing inexorably, according to an internal dialectic, to a final idealised state, where society had realised itself completely in terms of its socio-political goals of egalitarianism and an end to economic exploitation. History fell into a pattern for such thinkers and could be turned to account ideologically by those aware of the nature of its internal workings. For Marx it was a class war being fought down through the ages and support for the working class would eventually bring this to a triumphant conclusion: the dictatorship of the proletariat, who would now control all the means of production, ensuring that the profits these generated were shared equally in the public interest rather than capitalists hiving off most of those profits for themselves. This was to be the Marxist version of 'Freedom' and to resist it, as the establishment predictably did, was to be on the wrong side of history; to be a communist was to have made the correct moral decision. Marx's is a philosophy of dissent in that campaigning sense – and one prepared to go to the extent of being a 'philosophy of defiance' in Howard Caygill's formulation[8] – given that it is underpinned by a strong sense of social justice. It offers a devastating critique of a socio-political system that still resonates through to the present day and the effects of neoliberalism and globalisation on the international economy. Profit still ends up with the few rather than the many, in some cases in what are barely imaginable amounts to the average individual, measured out in billions of dollars, pounds or euros, as with high-profile technological entrepreneurs or social media platform-owners. The Marxist dialectic is system-building with a very specific ideological purpose, infused with strong ethical concerns that almost anyone on the left would be happy to support (even if not its programme for implementing these).

It is when this campaigning dissent is subordinated to a totalising overall philosophical system, itself taken to be beyond criticism of any kind, that problems start. What Marxism does not allow for, certainly in its communist adaptation, is any serious questioning of its authority, turning it into just another monolithic grand narrative geared to suppressing opposition and resisting change.[9] Gaining power is its overriding objective. The concern of true believers is implementation of the theory, not analysis of it. Hence their hostile reaction to post-Marxism, which started to ask some very awkward questions indeed of the Marxist establishment about its consistent failure to live up to the promise of its claims – even after revolutions guaranteeing its political supremacy in both Russia and China, giving it control over a very substantial portion of the global population. It is worth noting, however, that just as democracies can die, so can grand narratives, which is all the justification dissent, in whatever form it might take, needs to continue speaking out to those in power to point out their defects. System-building has its limits too, as Soviet communism eventually discovered, although admittedly it took several generations to do so and left a legacy of authoritarianism that has proved difficult to overcome in Russian politics. Scepticism wants to induce doubt in the minds of system-builders before they carry their theories to those limits, and questioning the assumptions they make in constructing their arguments is the obvious place to start that process.

Questioning their basic assumptions, such as whether there actually is such a thing as an identifiable force working through history with its particular trajectory, is an even more obvious point to make in the context of both Hegel and Marx. What if this is no more than a hypothesis? How could it ever be conclusively proved not to be? The notion that the end of the dialectic could be so neatly specified as both Hegel and Marx believed has also been called into question, with Theodor W. Adorno arguing in *Negative Dialectics* that it would simply go on generating new contradictions, that any proposed ending could only be arbitrary. There was no end to the process, no end to history, with Adorno insisting that 'a total philosophy is no longer to be hoped for', a scathing assessment to make of the system-building imperative in general and Marxism in particular.[10] John Medearis's insistence that democracy must always be 'oppositional' in character is broadly similar to Adorno's notion of an open-ended dialectic.[11] Internal tensions and competing worldviews will keep occurring, that is just in the nature of social existence; democracy is to be thought of, therefore, as 'an inspiring but perpetually troubled endeavor, a difficult, ongoing struggle with no clear outcome in sight'.[12] Bonnie Honig also emphasises the necessarily oppositional nature of democratic politics, in contrast to the more consensus-minded goals of political theory which she does not feel reflect the reality of political life. For her, that reality is a 'perpetual contest, even within an ordered setting'.[13] We cannot therefore expect any resolution along the lines of a Marxist utopia where all such struggle has been conclusively overcome; that can only be achieved as it was under communism, by outlawing dissent and imposing totalitarian rule on the population at large. Honig warns against any such 'displacement of politics' by theory, arguing that we should embrace instead the 'ruptures and uncertainties that mark democratic politics'.[14]

Calling the historical dialectic a hypothesis is a textbook example of telling those in authority what they do not want to hear, and poststructuralist and postmodernist thinkers are always ready to take up that challenge. Religions are just as vulnerable to that charge of being based on a hypothesis. There is no conclusive proof for the existence of any divinity whatsoever, which has to raise questions about the authority that religious hierarchies have always claimed. Scepticism is at its most powerful when it homes in on system-building's initial assumption; that is where systems are at their most vulnerable. It soon becomes apparent that systems rely very heavily on attracting a community of believers who are willing to take what its leaders say on trust (another example of almost reflex suspension of disbelief). Success in doing so, however, and building up a tradition to augment it (which religions in particular lay so much weight on), will never amount to philosophical proof; neither will sacred books such as the Bible or the Koran.

In defence of philosophers, it has to be pointed out that even if they are not sceptics, they do demand proof of what their peers are claiming in their theories. Sceptics are just that bit more probing, and no doubt irritating, in pushing that demand back to the very first step in constructing the system, but the discipline as a whole has far stricter criteria in dealing with arguments than, say, politics does – that elusive starting point excepted. Philosophers are not as likely as politicians to be conspiracy theorists either, so being sceptical is not to be taken as being anti-philosophical. Even if their critics can accuse them of that, postmodernists and poststructuralists should not be classified that way either, which is the next topic for discussion.

Postmodernist and poststructuralist dissent

The postmodern and poststructuralist movements have brought dissent back into philosophical discourse with a crusading zeal, particularly with respect to the issue of meaning. There is an unmistakably sceptical cast to such thought, which rejects the notion that meaning can be pinned down in any given language exchange. For Jacques Derrida that assumption permeates all of Western philosophical history (the 'metaphysics of presence', as he dubs it), and once it is called into question much of the authority of that tradition effectively disappears. It is a typically sceptical point that is being registered: Western philosophy has no ground that guarantees the truth of its propositions, nothing beyond all possible doubt on which to build a system of thought or belief with confidence that it will hold (again, it is largely tradition that is maintaining the system). In Derrida's analysis language is, as he puts it, a 'field . . . of play' rather than a set of fixed meanings that pin down words precisely.[15] Ambiguities and slippages of meaning are therefore to be taken as the norm; there is no such thing as straightforward transmission of meaning, whether in verbal or written form. Any word is capable of triggering an association of ideas in the individual which will be unique to him or her: the play of language taking over, as it always will. Given this endless play, the result is that as far as Derrida is concerned the Western tradition of philosophy, in fact Western thought in general, is based on assumptions that lie beyond proof. Structuralism provides a particularly pertinent example of what this involves for him. The notion of structure itself only works 'by a process of giving it a center or of referring to it as a point of presence, a fixed origin' – the metaphysics of presence in action.[16] Assuming that fixed origin is what makes system-building possible, as it did in structuralism with its notion of a 'deep structure' dictating how systems operated, but it has no underlying reality; it is as if any system derived from it is built on sand. There is no ultimate moment of presence to guarantee any of the system's claims; it is a mere convention to proceed as if there is, putting a large question mark over not just structuralism but the entire edifice of Western thought – dissent at its most provocative. The complex grammars that thinkers like Roland Barthes constructed for various discourses (literature, film and advertising, for example) depend upon there being a deep structure; take that away and there is no basis for structuralism as a movement.[17]

It is small wonder that Derrida aroused so much hostility in the philosophical world, although it is worth pointing out that the ambiguity he draws attention to in discourse is something that creative writers, and particularly poets, revel in. Some of the most interesting work that has come out of deconstruction has been in literary criticism, with poetry – an area where ambiguity and slippage of meaning are deliberately cultivated by practitioners – a popular topic.[18] For the more traditional type of philosopher, such as those trained in the analytical tradition in the English-speaking world, this is the very opposite of what they want to achieve in discourse: clarity of expression is what they are seeking instead. Locating the essence of what is meant by any statement is the objective of the analytical philosopher, while Derrida is denying that such an essence exists. There is no common ground between such outlooks and I concede that that can make deconstruction sound anti-philosophical in intent, unless you regard Derrida as a particularly radical sceptic out to challenge philosophers to reconsider the weak points of their assumptions and methods. Derrida puts it back to analytical philosophers to show that there is not as much play in discourse as he claims, and that to me sounds like an eminently philosophical task to pass on to them. At the very least it asks philosophers to look again at what they mean by essence and whether it is anything more than an unprovable hypothesis, along the lines of the Hegelian and Marxist dialectic perhaps.

A positive reading of Derrida's work would be to suggest that what it amounts to saying is that all linguistic exchanges, both spoken and written, are going to be subject to interpretation, and that those interpretations are going to vary, sometimes very dramatically (being 'within opinion' is another way of putting that). I doubt if his followers would accept that it is that straightforward, but it is a plausible way into the debate that has raged over deconstruction and what play might involve. Derrida's own writings have to be affected by play as well of course, which ought to give readers some latitude as to what they take from them. It would be misguided to consign deconstruction to the lunatic fringes of philosophy; it really does have something to add to the discipline's discourse, even if it can be irritatingly sweeping in its assertions (and I say this as one sympathetic to its overall aims).

One might even hazard a deconstructive critique of the storming of the US Capitol building by President Trump's supporters. In an emotionally charged speech that day, he urged them to go to the Capitol and protest against the Senate ratifying the results from each state for forming the Electoral College, because they were in Joe Biden's favour; they interpreted him as saying they should invade the building to stop the proceedings physically. His lawyers could claim that he never explicitly said to use physical force (and it is important to remember that there were several deaths recorded after the event, including one of the police staff defending the building); but on the other hand there was clearly enough play in the language he used in his speech for them to claim that their interpretation could be considered valid. He did say to 'fight like hell' to stop the process, but fight can mean both 'challenge' and 'attack'. What to Trump was rhetoric (giving him the benefit of the doubt, as enough Republican senators did in the subsequent impeachment trial to acquit him of the charge of sedition) was, to the angry mob of his supporters he was address-ing, a direct command from their head of state to be taken literally in the 'attack' sense. Several of those arrested went on to use that argument in their defence. I am not sure such a defence would persuade most juries and judges, however, especially if used to excuse violence. Being within opinion will only go so far in the courtroom. Perhaps that demonstrates the limits of deconstruc-tion, when real harm has been the consequence of language's field of play: at that point we have moved past philosophical critique, no matter how ingenious or intellectually diverting it may be.

As a consistently relativist-oriented thinker, Lyotard is no more willing to posit a fixed point of origin for philosophical thought and just as committed to taking up a dissenting position against its traditional assumptions. Authority in general is a permanent target for postmodernist and poststructuralist thinkers, who are unashamedly iconoclastic in that regard. Marxism, as a case in point, comes in for some severe criticism from Lyotard, as does every theory that can be described as a 'grand narrative'; that is, one with universalising tendencies that is convinced it is in posses-sion of the absolute truth about the nature of the world, such that its arguments are to be considered totally authoritative, negating the claims of all others. The Hegelian and Marxist systems have no loose ends in that sense; nothing is random, everything is con-nected and everything helps to prove the overall theory that the course of history is governed by an internal dialectic. Marxism presents itself as the ultimate grand narrative which removes the need for any other; the only one that understands the meaning of history. Lyotard, on the other hand, champions 'little narratives', movements with specific objectives that last only until these have been realised – until action has been taken over environmental abuses, for example. They are deliberately short-term and demar-cated in nature, therefore, not political ideologies in the generally understood sense (storming the Capitol would not count as one).

Grand narratives, such as Marxism or capitalist-based liberal democracy, may feel they can direct the course of history, but that is an illusion, one that has caused considerable harm to humanity. History unfolds without any of the specific patterns of the system-builders, with unforeseen events constantly intruding on even the most carefully worked-out plans of those in charge politically (pandemics being some of the most obvious examples, as all of us now know only too well from 2020 onwards). There is no end of history to work towards; the future is indeterminable, resistant to theoretical projections. Where Marx finds a pattern and an opportunity for his followers to maximise its impact by mobilising the proletariat against their exploiters, Lyotard finds only randomness, rendering system-building a pointless exercise. Events will always undermine the system's planning and can neither be predicted with any great accuracy – never mind as to the scale of their impact, another lesson to be learned from the pandemic – nor conclusively insured against; you must always be ready to improvise instead. Grand schemes of any kind are the antithesis to the poststructuralist or postmodernist worldview, which in that sense are not politics-friendly, given that planning on that scale is the motivating factor behind most of our politicians' careers.

Judgement becomes a problematic activity under Lyotard's relativism, because we have no basis on which to establish criteria for it that can be considered as lying beyond reasonable doubt and therefore able to hold over time (Lyotard once rather provocatively remarked that his criterion for making judgements was to have no criteria at all, the kind of comment that analytical philosophers can only think of as unprofessional[19]). System-builders such as Hegel and Marx assume such criteria and that leaves them open to challenge from sceptical thinkers in general, always on the lookout for an infinite regress. There is never a fixed starting point from which to establish such criteria or to guarantee the judgements that follow on from these, meaning that their legitimacy has to be open to doubt. Marxism is a theory very much concerned with making political judgements, styling itself as a definitive 'science of society', so it becomes very vulnerable to a sceptical critique. Granted, Lyotard is making judgements too, but their transitory nature is signalled by that admission of operating without fixed criteria.

His thought always remains tactical and oriented to the moment, resolutely opposed to being read as authoritative, as that would undermine the whole point of relativism.

Ernesto Laclau and Chantal Mouffe's *Hegemony and Socialist Strategy* took issue with Marxism's teleology, constituting a rallying cry for dissent within the Marxist movement. Their point was that the authoritarian side of Marxism was holding it back from realising how society was changing and thus failing to recognise where revolutionary ideas were emerging from in the later twentieth century. For these thinkers Marxism was too stuck in its ways to take advantage of any such changes that did not conform to its historical schema, rooted as this was in nineteenth-century cultural conditions and the particular class relations obtaining there: the product of heavy industry and a large exploited working class that has largely disappeared from Western society in a post-industrial age. They noted a tendency, too, for Marxists to rewrite history to fit their theories (fake news and alternative facts are by no means new phenomena). Accordingly, Laclau and Mouffe saw themselves as post-Marxists, more interested in the spirit than the letter of Marx's researches, his social criticism than his philosophical scheme, which they felt could no longer be defended.

In the academy, in the West anyway, Marxism has generated a wide range of approaches and interpretations, many varying quite considerably from the theory's original texts (even if still maintaining a faith in Marx's overall message[20]). Western Marxism, as it came to be called, was never as bound by the letter as classical Marxism was and helped to build up a momentum towards a post-Marxist outlook. Stuart Hall's work, as a case in point, was a catalyst for the development of cultural studies as an academic discipline with a distinctively Marxist inflection that has proved to be very influential.[21] Western Marxist thought could, therefore, be quite wide-ranging in its criticism of the movement's doctrines and it took much of its inspiration from Marx's pre-*Communist Manifesto* writings, such as the *Economic and Philosophic Manuscripts* of 1844 (not published until 1932). These gave a different picture of Marx than the one promoted in the communist world, a Marx with a much more liberal outlook.[22] But communism as a movement has always demanded solidarity of belief and thus has been constitutionally opposed to the notion of dissenting views on any aspect of Marxist theory. The party line is what takes precedence, and that is intrinsically inimical to the expression of any contrary opinions: unity is what is insisted upon and, when as rigorously applied as it was in communism, that is a principle which promotes the growth of dogmatism. As in monotheistic religions, there are things which must not be said (the reality of the dialectic is just not up for question), and punishment will be meted out to anyone who breaks that rule; to do so in the Soviet Union was to invite imprisonment at the very least. Post-Marxism represents an unashamed challenge to that mind-set, actively encouraging different interpretations and treating the theory, and its main texts, as a basis for social and political exploration, not as a definitive guide to understanding the world. Whereas internal dissent is anathema to classical Marxists, for Laclau and Mouffe it is the only way to save Marxist theory from declining into mere dogma, such that it can still act as an inspiration to future left-wing thought and action. The message behind their work is that the world has changed and so must Marxism, which seems an unobjectionable conclusion to draw – unless one is in thrall to a grand narrative, that is. Classical Marxists were distinctly unimpressed, however, dismissing Laclau and Mouffe as anti-Marxists without a proper sense of history or dialectics; dissent could only be understood as bad faith for that audience, for whom the dialectic was no mere hypothesis but a received truth about the nature of physical reality that could be scientifically proved (as will be discussed in more detail in Chapter 5).

While Laclau and Mouffe see a continuing relevance for Marxist theory, if appropriately amended and reinterpreted to take note of current cultural developments (which is where the arguments start with old-school Marxists), other post-Marxist thinkers have been less forgiving of Marxism's chequered history in the political domain. Lyotard, for example, rejects it out of hand as a tradition of thought that has long since outlived its usefulness and lost the confidence of much of the left (Jean Baudrillard made similar noises[23]). There is nothing worth saving from the Marxist corpus in Lyotard's opinion; it is just another flawed grand narrative, or universal theory, claiming, as usual quite unjustifiably, to have an explanation for everything – and a ready cure for everything. No such theory is possible for Lyotard since it allows for no views to the contrary, and he is a staunch defender of difference and diversity in our culture. A universal theory like Marxism is by definition authoritarian and totalitarian, therefore, and it would be a mistake to go on trying to recover insights from it for dealing with our contemporary political situation; in effect it is a misreading of our cultural development, which is never as straightforward as the grand-narrative mentality assumes it is. The necessity for dissent within any cultural framework becomes apparent whenever we find difference and diversity being overruled – and Marxism certainly does that, emphasising instead solidarity of belief and strict obedience to the party line. Scepticism becomes an appropriate method of resisting such practices, pointing out the unjustifiable assumptions that are involved when difference is denied recognition. System-building philosophy on the Marxist model has a tendency to forget this, hence the frustration exhibited by thinkers such as Lyotard, for whom it is an illegitimate use of philosophy. As he pointedly observes, '[y]ou can't be a philosopher (not even a teacher of philosophy) if your mind is made up on a question before you arrive' at a class or seminar; in other words, he does not want to deal in preconceived notions, but rather to let his thought develop and change as the discussion of the topic does.[24] Without dissent there is no philosophy for this thinker, for whom it is more an exercise in critique than a defence of supposedly universal truths or a method of establishing these.

Lyotard's concept of 'philosophical politics' indicates where he feels the system-builders go wrong, its objective being to open out debate as much as possible so that the voice of difference and diversity is always heard, that it is not restricted, as he so witheringly puts it, to 'the politics of "intellectuals" and of politicians'.[25] Intellectuals, in Lyotard's definition of them, are thinkers who provide support for ideological systems, defending their policies and rubbishing their critics, which for him is the exact opposite of what philosophers ought to be doing. Holding systems to account and pointing out their unwarranted assumptions, which is something all systems are guilty of making as far as sceptics in general are concerned, is what philosophical discourse should really be about. Systems invariably try to entrench themselves as firmly as possible, which leads naturally to blocking opportunities for dissent to question their motives. Scepticism is a permanent reminder of why we should not allow systems that degree of freedom, a reminder that systems need to be kept constantly under pressure if we are to frustrate their wish to exert domination over us, evidence of which is all around us from authoritarian politics down to the latest conspiracy theory. QAnon and philosophical scepticism could hardly be more incompatible.

The limits of scepticism

Scepticism does have its limits, however, and these are worth bearing in mind when assessing the role played by system-building in philosophy. The positive side of system-building is that it opens up new perspectives on politics and social existence that scepticism is not disposed to do; it wants to use philosophy to improve the quality of life and that is surely a laudable aim. For good or ill, depending on your ideological leanings, Marxism altered the socio-political landscape of the twentieth century very dramatically, prompting both Marxists and non-Marxists to keep thinking of new ways to approach political engagement. Without Marxism the world would most likely be a very different place and one has to take that into account when considering the value or otherwise of system-building. What scepticism reveals is that there is a dialectic within philosophical discourse between doubt and belief, and that these are in a symbiotic relationship with each other that sets the agenda for how that discourse develops. System-building is designed to make sense of the world of human affairs and it can inspire its followers with the belief that these can be altered for the better; it provides ideas for debate and there is always going to be a market for that. Scepticism provides a necessary corrective to some of the wilder claims that system-builders are prone to make (an explanation for everything when it comes to religions and universal theories such as Marxism), or the attitude of disdain they so often adopt towards criticism, but it is not as such a theory which can generate a programme for socio-political action.

System-builders have to answer the objections of the sceptics in order to improve their system, even if they can never render it foolproof to such critiques (there is always that issue of initial assumptions). Yet a philosophy based entirely on scepticism would be a rather impoverished discourse, as it can sometimes seem in the hands of poststructuralists and postmodernists – mere game-playing, as many of its critics see it (not always unjustifiably). There is an entirely defensible imperative within philosophy to open it out into the wider world so that it can effect change (a requirement of Marx himself, notably enough), be useful to the community at large in terms of ethics, politics, aesthetics – reasoning in general. It is only when that imperative feels it is beyond critique, in effect foolproof, that problems arise and that is where scepticism has to step in to point out the flaws in grand-narrative thinking. But societies have always been drawn towards grand narratives as a means of situating themselves in the world, whether aligning or differentiating themselves from others, and their success in enabling this has to be acknowledged. And just as we have to acknowledge that, so we have to recognise the limits of scepticism as well; philosophy would not be philosophy without it, but neither would it be without system-building, even if this does frequently require reining in. The discipline thrives on the resultant tension between the respective approaches.

Critical theory, dissent and authoritarianism

Poststructuralism and postmodernism were at the forefront of the so-called 'theory wars' in the university world of the 1980s and 1990s and these 'wars' can be very revealing about the complicated relationship between dissent and authoritarianism in intellectual circles, as well as of the limits of scepticism. Critical theory became an area of intense debate in the humanities in this period and those debates could get very acrimonious indeed. From structuralism onwards critical theories, which drew heavily on philosophical discourse, made a huge impact on all the critical disciplines in the humanities and social sciences, with each new 'ism' that came along generating enthusiastic supporters and just as many vociferous detractors. Structuralism's claims were dismantled by poststructuralists, most particularly by Derrida's theory of deconstruction, modernism's by postmodernists. Feminism adapted both these theories (as well as post-Marxism) to its own concerns in its critique of patriarchy, noting a distinct lack of difference and diversity in its beliefs or a commitment to addressing these seriously; postcolonialism went on to do the same. New theorists came and went, each offering a new perspective which seemed to demand that academics took sides, for or against the 'ism' in question, in what were effectively long-running philosophical debates about such basic concerns as the nature of truth and meaning.

The line taken by deconstructionists was that their theory overturned not just structuralism, by then a well-entrenched critical method, particularly in France, but the entire corpus of Western philosophy, the argument being that the latter was based on the assumption that meaning could be unproblematically communicated from speaker to speaker, that there was an inherent stability to language that users could depend on. Since for Derrida language was characterised not by fixed, determinate meanings but by indeterminacy, meaning was always in a state of play and that rendered universal theories, of truth or anything else, invalid. The implications of that position soon became clear in literature departments, where adherents to deconstruction set about challenging the critical enterprise on which the discipline of literary studies was founded, leaving many to wonder if there even was a basis for literary criticism any more. Both sides became very dogmatic about their beliefs, with little in the way of middle ground being acknowledged. Their views excluded each other's, with the traditionalists accusing the new breed of critical theorists of charlatanism, almost a default position in such situations, although one that inevitably closes down meaningful dialogue. Any humanities academic who attended conferences during the theory wars will remember the rancour that so often prevailed and cast a pall over the proceedings; it was a culture war within the profession that has still not entirely died out. Philosophy departments in the UK were initially very resistant to the new continental philosophy, although the subject slowly crept on to the syllabus in many of them, even if it was with grudging acceptance much of the time (and I have personal, rather painful, experience of the negotiations this could involve, with the complaint from senior colleagues being that 'this was just not philosophy').

To those outside the academy the theory wars seemed like so much pointless game-playing, however, and deconstruction came in for much mockery as an irrational theory which seemed to render ordinary discourse all but impossible. The serious philosophical points that poststructuralists and postmodernists were raising tended to get lost in the process, even though they were, and still are, of considerable intellectual importance, with far wider social and political implications than they are generally credited with having. At issue was whether any system, of thought or belief, could ever be anything other than arbitrary; that is, based on unsubstantiated assumptions. There are still ways round this problem, of preferring some beliefs to others even if they have no absolute foundation that ensures they are beyond all possible doubt (weighing up their advantages and disadvantages in everyday situations, for example, as Richard Rorty recommends[26]); but most of the time it is just avoided and the assumptions in question taken for granted.

Conclusion: scepticism v. grand narratives

Dissent is well represented in contemporary philosophy therefore, although it has no lack of detractors there, its radical scepticism ruffling many feathers in its rejection of received wisdom in the field in terms of its assumptions, beliefs and working methods. Scepticism tends to annoy those in authority wherever it applies itself, and all discourses have their system-builders and true believers who do not take kindly to being challenged as to the validity of their epistemological foundations or the conclusions reached on the basis of these. It is a criticism often directed at poststructuralist and postmodernist thinkers that they are negative and even nihilistic in their analyses (both Derrida and Lyotard have been singled out on this score), but there is a philosophical justification for their attack on the pretensions of grand narratives and the authority they are allowed to wield in our culture. Unless grand narratives are put under pressure in this deliberately provocative way, then their natural tendency is to accrue as much power to themselves as they can by systematically marginalising all dissenting voices in their field of operation. We are by no means always within opinion as far as the authorities are concerned, unless of course the opinion is their own, which is not to be questioned (not that they would ever concede to it being described as mere opinion, nor subject to the endless play that Derrida claims it is fated to be). It is this imperialistic imperative in grand narratives that poststructuralist and postmodernist philosophy is concerned to undermine and they deserve credit for their efforts in the cause of an anti-authority dissent. To make the authorities feel uncomfortable about the justification (or lack of it) for their policies is to perform a public service, one that all sceptics would want to encourage unreservedly throughout our society, at both the formal and informal level. It does not matter what the field is, its authority figures should never be allowed to escape scrutiny or the requirement to justify their actions to the public – and on a regular basis. Anything that ensures that is surely worth supporting.

Notes

1. Lyotard and Thébaud, *Just Gaming*, p. 43.
2. Lyotard, *Discourse, Figure*, p. 14.
3. See works such as Lukács, *History and Class Consciousness*; Gramsci, *Selections from the Prison Notebooks*.
4. I cover the development of post-Marxism as a movement in more detail in Sim, *Post-Marxism*, where I trace a range of internal critiques of Marxism back to the theory's early days.
5. Hegel, *The Philosophy of History*, p. 457.
6. See Schopenhauer, *Essays and Aphorisms*, for a basic outline of his philosophical pessimism.
7. Ibid., p. 54.
8. See Caygill, *On Resistance*.
9. For grand narrative, see Lyotard, *The Postmodern Condition*.
10. Adorno, *Negative Dialectics*, p. 136.
11. See Medearis, *Why Democracy Is Oppositional*.
12. Ibid., p. 1.
13. Honig, *Political Theory and the Displacement of Politics*, p. 15.
14. Ibid., pp. 2, 4.

15. Derrida, *Writing and Difference*, p. 289.
16. Ibid., p. 278.
17. See, for example, Barthes, *Image Music Text*.
18. See, for example, the work of the so-called Yale School (Harold Bloom, Paul de Man, Geoffrey Hartman and J. Hillis Miller), all of whom fell under the influence of Derrida. Their collective production, *Deconstruction & Criticism*, offers a useful introduction to their work, with Hartman arguing that '[t]he separation of philosophy from literary study has not worked to the benefit of either' (p. ix).
19. See Lyotard and Thébaud, *Just Gaming*, p. 18.
20. See, for example, Eagleton, *Why Marx Was Right*. Terry Eagleton absolves Marx of most of the major objections to his work, and, while conceding that Marx sometimes could get things wrong, insists that his thought has been 'travestied' by most of his critics (p. 239).
21. See, for example, Hall, *Essential Essays, vol. 1*.
22. See Marx, *Early Writings*.
23. See Baudrillard, *The Mirror of Production*.
24. Lyotard, *The Postmodern Explained to Children*, p. 116.
25. Lyotard, *The Differend: Phrases in Dispute*, p. xiii.
26. See Rorty, *Consequences of Pragmatism*, p. 138.

Chapter 4

Religious Dissent

Historically speaking, monotheisms have tended to be very harsh on the notion of dissent, treating almost any opposition to their authority as heretical and therefore all but demanding extreme punishment to be dealt out (as with the Inquisition, for example) to deter others from following suit. Uncritical belief is what religious leaders seek to maintain at all times and that allows little, if any, scope for alternative interpretations of the relevant doctrines and sacred works which go to make up their theology: conformity is always the monotheistic goal, to be pursued as vigorously as one's culture permits. Once up and running, intolerance is the house style in such cases, with tradition becoming the arbiter of what can be said or done doctrinally. Militant authoritarianism tends to create resentment of those in power, however, and that is where dissent comes into play. Protestantism is a prime example of that process, constituting a dissenting movement against what it took to be the abuse of power and authority within Catholicism, a division which led to war and conflict throughout Christian Europe for several generations (and still does in places like Northern Ireland). Protestantism itself soon broke down into a range of competing positions, each claiming to be the definitive reading of Christian doctrine, resulting in yet more conflict. An interesting case study of how this operated can be found in the development of Nonconformism within the Anglican Church in the sixteenth and seventeenth centuries, a movement that came to be known as Dissent and its followers collectively as Dissenters. It provides a classic example of the clash between authority and dissent, particularly of the intransigence of authority when faced with any concerted challenge to its power base and the belief system that it has established. A classic example, too, of how dissent tends to turn against opposition to its own power once it attains authority and autonomy itself. Large-scale organisations are rarely well disposed towards dissent, generally treating it as a nuisance to be quashed as quickly as possible; power is jealously guarded by those at the top in any such set-up, whether religious or corporate.

I am not religious, although dissenting religion, particularly Puritanism, has been a long-term research interest of mine, going back to my days as a doctoral student.[1] Various religious positions are discussed below, but I am not as such biased towards any of them in strictly theological terms, not arguing the merits of any one over the others, nor attempting an exhaustive analysis of the belief systems involved; being sceptical of religious belief in general, that would not be appropriate on my part (just for the record, however, I should own up to being a Protestant atheist, Scots Presbyterian variety). If I am drawn here to a figure such as John Bunyan, it is because of his literary talent rather than his work's religious message, although his spirited resistance to political authority is also a significant part of that attraction (hence his appearance at various other points in the book as well). The chapter is therefore to be considered a case study in the evolution of opposition to authority and the response of the latter to dissenting voices from within its own field, which is rarely very positive, as working through some of its main historical instances soon reveals. Religion happens to be an area where this clash brings out some of the worst instincts in authority, which is generally in a state of denial about the possibility that other interpretations of its doctrine could have their own validity, or that they may be as entitled to set up their own system as the existing hegemonic authority was in the first place. Dissent is instead almost always viewed as a threat and it is the consequences of this that I am concerned to explore, the culture that intolerance generates in its bid to maintain total control. (Judaism was, however, allowed to exist to some extent in both the Christian and Islamic realms in the medieval and early modern periods, although persecution was common and anti-Semitism widespread. It is toleration only in a very limited sense.)

Pre-Protestant dissent

Christianity had its share of challenges to central authority long before Protestantism came on the scene, with various heresies developing and testing the power of the ruling Catholic Church. A particularly notable one was Catharism, 'the most notorious heresy of all time' as it has been described, and it came to attract very considerable popular support in the medieval period.[2] To the Catholic Church hierarchy dissent was heresy and it could be brutal in suppressing dissent as a threat to its power, which by this stage in the organisation's history had become very substantial, both socially and politically. Its hierarchy was to be the sole judge of what constituted doctrinal correctness and there were to be no deviations at all from this. In Jean-François Lyotard's frame of reference this is an entirely typical example of grand-narrative behaviour, of its inability to countenance difference and diversity, to be an open rather than a closed system. (As far as religion went, Lyotard spoke favourably of paganism as in the case of classical Greece, where there was no one overall divine authority and a considerable amount of local variation in beliefs and practices.[3]) The party line rules instead and it tends to stick closely to its traditions, which eventually will clash with social and political changes in its world, stoking up resentment against the system's innate dogmatism and demand for obedience from its followers. All major religions have to go through this and they rarely handle it all that well. It was in precisely such a situation that first Catharism and then later Protestantism sought to make a case for a new interpretation and organisation of Christian belief. It may take time to develop, but dissent will always emerge against traditional authority and the latter never really seems to learn from that history, almost invariably responding with intolerance.

While that stance was enough to see off Catharism in time, it would signally fail with Protestantism.

Catharism's stronghold was the Languedoc region of France where, as one writer on the movement has put it, it had become 'virtually the dominant religion' by the early thirteenth century.[4] Cathars developed a distinctive doctrinal system, complete with its own priestly hierarchy (deemed to have reached the condition of being 'perfect'), and accompanying rituals. All of this put Catharism severely at odds with the medieval Catholic Church, which felt compelled to take action to reassert its claim to sole authority over Christendom in the West (Eastern Christianity in the Orthodox tradition had its own share of dissenting sects to deal with, such as the Bogomils in Bulgaria). The fact that Cathars were in favour of the Bible being translated into the vernacular and made available to all believers was a further source of irritation to the Catholic hierarchy, who wanted it to be kept restricted to the priesthood, since that granted it powerful control over the faithful as mediators of God's word. When Protestantism came on the scene a few centuries later, Biblical translation was again to become one of the most critical points of contention, an issue that Catholicism could never quite keep out of theological discussion.

The Cathars were ruthlessly hunted down and their system dismantled, their main sin being to have developed a different interpretation of Christianity based on Manichean principles, which postulated that there was both a good and an evil god locked in conflict in the universe (a belief shared by the Bogomils[5]). For a Catholic Church committed to monotheism and an omnipotent god, that could only be defined as heresy and thus worthy of a crusade, which eventually succeeded in destroying the Cathar system. Unleashing a crusade against a Christian population indicates just how grave the Catholic hierarchy considered the situation to be: the intransigence of authority could hardly go further than this. What the episode also revealed, however, was that dissenting theological views could exert considerable appeal and that Catholic authoritarianism was very vulnerable to this; Catharism did, after all, hold sway in its home region for quite a considerable length of time, becoming highly symbolic in that regard. Nor was it the last challenge to Catholic authoritarianism before the rise of Protestant reform, with Lollards and Hussites also proving a trial to the Catholic hierarchy. Each time around it was very much a case of dissenters speaking to a future age, rather than being bogged down in tradition, which was Catholicism's default position. Powerful a force as tradition is, and manipulable as such by the ruling authorities in any field, it can be challenged successfully if dissent keeps building up momentum, and excessive dogmatism certainly fuels that. Neither was this just a religious issue, because the church was deeply involved in politics throughout the period being discussed – being temporal as well as spiritual rulers in central Italy, for example (the 'Papal States'). Religious anti-authoritarianism always had a political dimension.

The Lollard movement flourished in the fourteenth century in England and was particularly critical of the papacy, to the point of accusing the pope of being the Antichrist (Catharism had made similar accusations and it is to crop up throughout the history of Protestantism into our own day). As Richard Rex has noted, in its day the term 'lollard' simply meant 'heretic', whereas to historians like him now, it refers to a 'distinct, if somewhat broad, band of dissident beliefs and practices' that were inspired by the work of the theologian John Wyclif.[6] Discontent with church policy was there to be worked on by the reform-minded, simmering away just under the surface of Catholic culture. Wyclif was in fact charged with heresy by the authorities, although never formally punished for it. Lollardism was yet another movement that was in favour of the scriptures being made available to all in the vernacular, a notion which was increasingly creating difficulties for the Catholic hierarchy. Anti-Catholic dissent had a democratic feeling to it in its commitment to opening up biblical knowledge to the wider public, as well as in its campaign against dogmatism and power exercised from the top down.

Hussites followed the teachings of the Bohemian theologian Jan Hus (although they tended to be more radical in their beliefs than Hus himself was[7]) and became enough of a force to prompt crusades against them by the Catholic Church, as the Cathars had in their turn. Hus was burned at the stake for heresy in 1415, but the movement carried on after his death, supporting such radical ideas as lay preaching (later to become so popular amongst sectarians in seventeenth-century England, with John Bunyan as one of the most prominent exponents), which represented a very direct challenge to the power of the priesthood and its control of scriptural knowledge. Opposition to Catholicism's social and political domination kept breaking through until the Reformation finally succeeded in creating a viable alternative to Catholic hegemony, one that has stood the test of time.

Protestant dissent

From Martin Luther onwards, Protestantism took dissent to a point much further than its forebears in the pre-Protestant age had ever managed, generating a new range of theologies which Catholicism, despite its best efforts, failed to suppress as it had always been able to do in the past. The Cathars may have been defeated (and with considerable brutality) but the burgeoning reform movement initiated by Luther proved to be an altogether tougher and more determined opponent, firmly committed to undermining Catholic authoritarianism through a theology offering greater personal access to the scriptures. Luther's Ninety-Five Theses represented a very explicit attack on the abuses of power that the church was guilty of, prompting a wider expression of dissent that even Catholic authoritarianism could not contain. Lutheranism and Calvinism both flourished and in turn gave rise to various other interpretations of Christian doctrine, as the rise of Puritanism in late sixteenth-century England notably demonstrated. It was a process that was to continue for several centuries as the Protestant community kept dividing ever further: protest against authority seems to be hard-wired into the Protestant mentality. Although it now tolerates the existence of other Christian sects, Catholicism still considers itself to be the only true interpretation of Christianity and it wields greater power internationally than Protestantism does, both financially and politically; but Protestantism's impact socially and politically over the centuries makes a very good case for the value of dissent. Catholicism itself had to change its ways to meet the Protestant challenge and responded with the Counter-Reformation, which did away with many of the practices, such as indulgences, that had brought it into such disrepute. Dissent had long since made its point, however, and was not to be stopped this time around.

One of Protestantism's key objectives in undermining the power of the Catholic hierarchy was to make the Bible available to believers in their vernacular language, a policy that led to greater dissent against the established religious order and the dogma it was propounding. The mediation of the priesthood that Catholicism insisted upon was thereby reduced, meaning that the grand narrative they represented began to lose some of its authority, encouraging dissenting viewpoints to be expressed. Those viewpoints could use the Bible against the Catholic hierarchy, further undermining its domination of belief in Christendom. From the Cathars onwards, Bible translation was a bitterly contested issue within Western Christendom, one that Catholicism recognised as posing a considerable threat to its control over believers. It is through knowledge of the Bible gained from intensive reading of it in English, for example, that figures like Bunyan could justify their opposition to authority, this time around from the state-sponsored Anglican Church, as will be discussed below. To a dissenter, the Bible was the ultimate authority and the priesthood very much secondary to it; hence the recourse of so many dissenters like Bunyan to quoting scripture at length (sometimes quite inordinate length, to browbeat their opponent) in any confrontation. The rise of lay preaching in the period indicated just how subversive to the established theological order such knowledge could be, doing away with the overall hierarchical structure on which that order depended. Bunyan and his ilk could appear from anywhere, evading central control as they went about their business, following the dictates of their conscience rather than a party line drawn up by the authorities. For their part, the authorities more or less went to war against what they considered to be 'the overscrupulous consciences of separatists' in the Restoration period, although ultimately to no avail.[8] Dissent proved to be a very resilient opponent.

The rise of Puritanism

Puritanism started as a reform movement within the Anglican Church in the late sixteenth century, when it was still developing its own theological system in the wake of Henry VIII's break with Rome. The break was undertaken for political rather than doctrinal reasons, the new church styling itself as Anglo-Catholic and even retaining some elements of Catholicism in its services; but it soon gave rise to internal debate about matters of doctrine in the form of Puritanism, which bitterly resented the presence of any Catholic elements at all in worship and became more and more vocal on the issue in the aftermath of Henry's reign. By then Protestantism was already a force to be reckoned with on the European continent and it is not surprising that its ideas and doctrines came to attract attention in England. Calvinist theology, for example, soon had its supporters and many of the sects that were to break away from the Anglican Church in the seventeenth century, such as the Baptists, were strongly influenced by it. Such groups came to be labelled Dissenters, or Nonconformists, and they went on to play a critical role in English political life of the period, particularly in the Civil War of the 1640s and then the Commonwealth republic that ruled the country between 1649 and 1660. It was dissenting Puritans who founded the colony in Massachusetts, thus giving them an equally important role in the subsequent development of the American state.

Dissent was a direct challenge to the authority of the English ruling class, serious enough to lead to the beheading of King Charles I in 1649 after a dissent-inspired Parliament had triumphed over the Royalist side in the Civil War, going on to turn England into a republican state under the eventual leadership of Oliver Cromwell as Lord Protector. Although the monarchy was restored in 1660, after the death of Cromwell and the swift collapse of his son Richard's ill-fated attempt at government as his successor, dissent was still to be a significant factor in English life, a movement that the ruling authorities never quite managed to suppress altogether, thus damaging the image they wanted to present. Anglicanism may have had the status of a state church, but it was never to have the complete control of religious worship that it sought and indeed considered to be its right as England's established church; dissenting consciences held firm. The government did, however, do its best to impose conformity of belief in the nation, passing various laws to prohibit worship outside the established church, such as the Act of Uniformity in 1662, which resulted in hundreds of clergymen refusing to obey its dictates and thus being forced out of their positions. Many of them continued to hold services in secret afterwards, but with the threat of arrest if found out by the authorities, which could lead to charges of 'riotous assembly' and imprisonment under the terms of the Conventicle Acts of 1664 and 1670; yet another 'law and order' response to a protest. The Five Mile Act of 1665 also excluded rejected ministers from being any closer than that distance to their previous site of services: theological social distancing, one might say. 'Restoration England', as Mark Goldie has observed, 'was a persecuting society.'[9] Yet despite such constant harassment, dissenting ministers went on defying the government and preaching where and when they could manage, supported by loyal congregations just as determined to resist official pressure to conform. Even such a highly regarded minister of the period as Richard Baxter, a noted moderate within the Anglican establishment who enjoyed royal support in the early days of the Restoration settlement (briefly serving as Charles II's chaplain, for example), could not bring himself to follow the government line and had to step down. That was the end of neither Puritanism nor religious dissent in England, however, as the subsequent career of Bunyan will demonstrate. 'Overscrupulous consciences' just kept on coming to the fore to confound the plans of the authorities, undaunted by the threat of fines or imprisonment (as Baxter was to suffer, like Bunyan).

The dissenting lifestyle: John Bunyan

Bunyan provides an excellent example of the dissenting temperament, both in his life and in his writings; his uncompromising, conscience-led opposition to the political authorities, with their insistence on religious uniformity, is very symbolic in this respect.

The Pilgrim's Progress offers a fascinating psychological as well as sociological profile of the dissenting lifestyle and its struggle to maintain itself in the unsympathetic cultural environment of Restoration England, such that its message has reverberated down the centuries, keeping the Puritan spirit alive in the public mind (backed up by a running commentary of biblical citation in its extensive marginalia to reinforce its Nonconformist, unmistakably anti-establishment, stance).[10] Bunyan's autobiography, *Grace Abounding to the Chief of Sinners*, is no less revealing of the internal struggle that the dissenter had to go through to maintain his faith, as well as the many emotionally destabilising ups and downs it could involve. Despite the obstacles and temptations placed in his path, including having to fight a pitched battle with the fearsome demon Apollyon, as well as the periodic doubts and understandable anxieties he is assailed by as to the justification for his arduous journey to the Celestial City (leaving wife and children behind him in the City of Destruction), *The Pilgrim's Progress*'s protagonist Christian manages to keep going until he is received into Heaven as one of the saved 'elect'. Bunyan had earlier shown the same degree of commitment to his dissenting religious beliefs by refusing to give up lay preaching in the early stages of the Restoration period when it had been declared an illegal action by the new monarchical regime, in which the Anglican Church was asserting itself again to the detriment of all dissenting believers. Pressed hard by the court after his arrest for the offence to give such a promise and stick to his trade as a tinker, Bunyan's defiant response was:

> I durst not make any further promise: for my conscience would not suffer me to do it. And again, I did look upon it as my duty to do as much good as I could, not only in my trade, but also in communicating to all people wheresoever I came, the best knowledge I had in the Word.[11]

The rebellious side of dissent comes through very strongly at such points; individual conscience took precedence over political power and refused to give in to its demands, no matter what the cost to the individual's welfare – or that of his family either. Bunyan was to be imprisoned for a period of twelve years, yet on his release was to continue with his preaching activities (and very successfully too, being able to draw large crowds to his services). He displayed the same cast of mind that the determined whistle-blower has to cultivate to stand up to the authorities.

Persecution of dissenters largely ended after the 'Glorious Revolution' of 1688–9 when the Stuart monarchy was over-thrown and it became possible openly to worship in a sectarian church.[12] Various restrictions were imposed on dissenters: politics and the law were off limits to them as careers, for example, as was study at the universities of Oxford and Cambridge, meaning they could not gain a theology degree as a route into the priesthood. Nevertheless, religious freedom was more or less assured from that point onwards; dissent had won that particular battle by refusing to give in to severe repression from the government, Bunyan being a potent symbol of its determination to go its own way regardless of the consequences. Henceforth, the Anglican Church had to co-exist alongside a series of sectarian churches, each with its own distinctive theology and loyal congregations. Those who came to disagree with any particular sectarian theology because of their differing interpretation of the Bible could, if they felt strongly enough about it, start a new church of their own – and this did happen on several occasions. Dissent had succeeded in altering the religious landscape of the country; there was now religious pluralism in operation – although Catholics were to be excepted from this arrangement for quite some time (even Protestant dissent having its limits over that issue).

Fundamentalism and dissent

Fundamentalist movements can be found in all religions and they are resolutely opposed to dissent, which tends to be treated as if it were an insult to their faith: to question that is to question their divinity and their entire history. Denialism is in full operation in such cases. Islamic fundamentalism is currently the most active form of fundamentalism (certainly in political terms of reference) and considers itself to be engaged in a holy war, *jihad*, against the entire rest of the world, convinced that its God is the only true God, its sacred work the only source of wisdom. While these are fairly standard fundamentalist assumptions for monotheisms, not all of them interpret fundamentalism quite as seriously in the twenty-first century as Islamists do. Infidels effectively have no rights at all as far as radical Islam is concerned, hence the various terrorist acts their many groups (al-Qaida, Isis etc.) have carried out internationally in the last few decades, designed to show the depth of their faith since in many cases they take the form of suicide bombings. Opposition to what is taken to be dissent against your belief system can hardly be taken much further than sacrificing your own life in its service.

The coronavirus pandemic was a gift to fundamentalists across the religious spectrum, enabling them to claim that it had to be a case of divine punishment for humankind's sinning ways. Both Christian and Islamic fundamentalists took this line, arguing that it was an expression of God's anger at humanity's lapse from his teachings. It would seem that not much has changed from the days of the plague for theologians of this stripe, who can turn any crisis to their preaching advantage: God's will covers all eventualities and the devout will fully accept that explanation as authoritative. Some Islamic fundamentalists also claimed that the pandemic was deliberately created and released by the West, seen as a source of endless evil for the more radical of these (yet another conspiracy theory to add to the list); an example of what happens when you do not embrace Islam, the only true religion. For such thinkers, God is most certainly not tolerant of dissent from following his will to the letter, and periodic pandemics are designed to jolt us into realising what is wrong with our lifestyle, a harsh but necessary reminder of the limitations of our power. God is not a pluralist in this regard; there is one, and only one, true way to live and we deviate from it at our peril. Monotheistic fundamentalists of all persuasions can fully agree with that sentiment, while refusing to allow each other the right to do so; fundamentalism is an exclusive club, with strict entry qualifications.

The politics that follows on from such beliefs is just as unforgiving, just as inimical to even the suggestion of pluralism. Theocracy is its preferred option, as exists in several parts of the

Islamic world at present and has done in the Christian in the past (John Calvin's Geneva constitutes a notable example of how thorough and systematic this could be when taken in hand by zealots[13]). The overriding objective of a theocracy is to ensure the purity of religious belief and practice throughout the community, no variation at all being permitted; religious law is to be the basis of every social and political activity and the notion of religious freedom is completely rejected, counting only as heresy from such a strict perspective. Supporters of theocracy are to be found in the present-day Christian world as well, raising 'fears of "theocracy" reborn' amongst many liberals in the US, who are concerned at the increasing political power exercised by the religious right there.[14] American evangelicalism is as much a political as a religious movement, with very set views on how society should be run, and the Republican Party is particularly dependent on its support, which leaned heavily towards President Trump in the last two elections (with Trump himself claiming evangelical credentials, more than somewhat unconvincingly, it should be said, given his personal history). The authoritarian imperative is embedded in the fundamentalist psyche and does not acknowledge that there is any case to be made for difference and diversity in belief. Dissent is simply not on its agenda, counting as wilful refusal to acknowledge divine authority (the same can be said of secularism). Apply that attitude to politics and democracy is once again placed under significant threat.

The issue is complicated, however, by each interpretation of a monotheism considering itself to be the only correct one. It is a situation that occurs in Islam no less than in Christianity, with the split between its Sunni and Shia wings giving rise to considerable discord within the Islamic world – discord that can even run to armed conflict, yet another example of the unacceptable face of authority. Who has the most valid claim to be the true voice of a religion's fundamentals is a question that does seem to keep arising and creating problems within monotheisms. Strength of conviction rather than logical argument is what tends to carry the day in such cases and that makes it difficult to have any kind of philosophically inclined dialogue with fundamentalists, not that the latter would see much point in doing so anyway.

Religion and science

Grand narratives do not take kindly to any opposition to their worldview and religion is no exception. With regard to science, religions have often found it very hard indeed to go along with its theories – the case of Galileo being one of the most notorious examples of this trait. To the Catholic Church hierarchy he was dissenting against their conception of the universe, therefore against their religion and its sacred works. If the Bible gave one version of the nature of the universe and Galileo another, then the latter had to be wrong. To dissent from the Bible was to commit heresy and Galileo was forced to recant publicly, even if in private he adhered to his findings. This is always an option for those who fall foul of religious orthodoxy, but hardly one to further the progress of knowledge. Having to keep silent about your beliefs and your knowledge constitutes a victory for the authorities. Grand narratives do not like to see the fundamentals of their creed being challenged in any way at all and will exert whatever power they have to prevent that from ever occurring; preserving the system is valued over any advances made in the sciences. Science will always be in a subsidiary position to theology for religious leaders; there can be no contenders.

A prime instance of how theology overrules all other forms of knowledge for the fundamentalist mind can be found in the theory of creationism, which clashes very dramatically with science over the issue of the Earth's age and the evolution of life. Again, it is the Bible that generates the disagreement, with biblical literalism dictating what to believe about such issues. For creationists, a careful reading of the list of generations in the biblical narrative from Adam and Eve onwards adds up only to a few thousand years, therefore that must be the age of the Earth. Scientific evidence that it has to be several billion years old has to be discounted (as fake knowledge, presumably). Some other explanation for the apparent evidence has to be found, because the Bible could not be wrong: God might be testing our faith by seeing how we respond to apparently misleading information, or something along those lines. For all the contortions that such drastic telescoping of life's evolution involves – and they are very considerable indeed – there is a very sizeable constituency, particularly in the US, that follows the creationist line very faithfully. There is also a flourishing publishing industry to give the faithful everything they need to counter the scientific arguments that they will be confronted by, as browsing in a Christian bookshop will soon reveal. A popular, much reprinted example of creationist literature is Ken Ham's *The Lie: Evolution*, which argues that evolution is not a science but a religion – a false one, of course, because Christianity is the only true one. Faced with a choice between religion and science, the creationist faithful choose religion, taking on board Ham's message that 'Genesis [is] the Key to Defending Your Faith'.[15] It is yet another case of fake dissent, I would want to argue, and one that resonates unhelpfully through politics, as it manifestly does in America where the influence of the religious right is so extensive. If your opponents are lying about the Bible, then their word cannot be trusted about political matters either; evolution becomes a test of moral character, one that few non-evangelicals will pass. Scientific dissent is to be considered misguided, even heretical, by such fundamentalist believers. No compromise is possible between the respective viewpoints; for this constituency that would amount to a denial of the Bible, and that is definitely off limits for the fundamentalist Christian.

One does have to wonder, however, what would happen if evidence of life, in no matter how rudimentary a form it might be, were to be found elsewhere in our solar system, as is currently being speculated about Venus, plus several of the moons of other planets (and still considered a possibility of Mars's past, as various missions there tantalisingly suggest and will go on being programmed to search for). It would certainly not square with the biblical narrative: Genesis does not mention it. Written off as fake news perhaps? Or dismissed as a conspiracy by the scientific establishment to gain power and prestige for their enterprise? It is only fair to record that the data involved have since been queried by other research groups (that is in the nature of scientific enquiry); even so, they will no doubt continue to intrigue both scientists and theologians until a future Venus mission either confirms the finding or not.[16] While theology in a general sense can adapt to changing circumstances, and sometimes quite creatively too,

Biblical literalists would face an altogether more existential threat to their belief system by the discovery of extraterrestrial life, even if just at microbial level (which is considered the likeliest in terms of our own universe); uncritical belief does not go in for flexibility. Recent research suggests there are probably about five billion Earth-like planets in our Milky Way galaxy, which in turn is only one of an estimated several billion galaxies in the universe overall; this has to be considered the stuff of nightmares to the literalist mind.[17]

Conclusion: promoting difference and diversity

Religious belief has a complex relationship with dissent, therefore, sometimes promoting it, as Puritanism so notably did with such far-reaching socio-political effects, but more often refusing to listen to its arguments when they query its validity, as Cathars, Lollards and Hussites all found out in their turn when they tried to move away from the orbit of Catholicism. Since monotheistic religions tend towards the authoritarian in their manner, insisting on adherence to time-honoured doctrine as guarded and propounded by their respective hierarchies, that latter response is only to be expected; dissent is generally seen as a threat rather than an opportunity to reconsider, and possibly even to update, one's theology. Religions do change over time, but reluctantly at best and with little appetite for any significant reinterpretation of their core beliefs (as the saying goes, the Catholic Church thinks in terms of centuries on such matters). Maintaining traditional values is always seen as crucially important by religious hierarchies and there is a definitely conservative character to organised religion which works against the dissenting imperative: biblical literalism continues to exist because of that framework, five billion Earth-like planets in our home galaxy alone notwithstanding. What this means is that, as we shall see in Chapter 7, self-critique can become a problematic activity for the believer, undermined by the demands of the theological authorities (and I am taking self-critique to be an essential part of the dissenting temperament that I am making a case for). Nevertheless, dissent is vital to prevent religions becoming obstacles to social change, as they so often have proved to be in the past (and can be even now despite our more secular culture), and movements like Protestantism, especially in its early days, are to be applauded for enabling difference and diversity to play a role in religious discourse. That is a key concern of dissent in all discourses and why it ought to be given space to express itself, rather than being closed down by those in power; I find that to be a far more important factor in religious dissent than any of the theological differences lying behind it.

Looking at the history of religion enables us to see how authoritarianism and intolerance develop in an organisational or corporate context. The more traditionally conservative the institution is, then the greater the need for dissent to be there in dialogue, questioning its dogmatic outlook and calling for greater broadmindedness and a willingness to explore compromise (as well as putting the case for secularism). Hierarchies may not like it, choosing to relapse into denialism instead, but sectarianism is actually a sign of rude health in the religious arena: proof that belief is being tested, as sceptics will always recommend it should be, whatever area of human endeavour we may be talking about. Nowhere is this more important than in science, the next area to be considered.

Notes

1. My PhD was the basis of my first book, *Negotiations with Paradox: Narrative Practice and Narrative Form in Bunyan and Defoe*.
2. O'Shea, *The Perfect Heresy*, p. 1.
3. 'What is important in the case of the Greeks is that their gods are not masters of the word in the sense in which the Christian God is a master of the word, that is, their word is not performative as the word of the Christian God is. It does not create the world, nor does it create any of the situations of the world' (Lyotard and Thébaud, *Just Gaming*, p. 39).
4. Martin, *The Cathars*.
5. Georgi Vasilev traces the connections between Orthodox and Western Christian sectarian movements in *Heresy and the English Reformation: Bogomil-Cathar Influence on Wycliffe, Langland, Tyndale and Milton*. Milton's Satan, often described as the most heroic figure in *Paradise Lost*, does seem to invite a Manichean reading of the work, there being, in Vasilev's opinion, a 'spiritual kinship' between Milton and the Bogomils (p. 117).

6. Rex, *The Lollards*, p. xii.
7. On this issue, see Kaminsky, *A History of the Hussite Revolution*, for whom the revolution the Hussites led was '*the* revolution of the later middle ages' (p. 1).
8. Goldie, 'The Theory of Religious Intolerance in Restoration England', p. 333.
9. Ibid., p. 331.
10. I discuss the continuing relevance of Puritan thought in our own time in Sim, *Twenty-First Century Puritanism: Why We Need It and How It Can Help Us*.
11. Bunyan, 'A Relation of the Imprisonment of Mr. John Bunyan', p. 92.
12. The history of religious toleration in the early modern/modern period has become a controversial topic in recent years. For a survey of the literature on this, see Collins, 'Redeeming the Enlightenment'.
13. For a detailed analysis of what this involved, see Kingdon with Lambert, *Reforming Geneva*.
14. Collins, 'Redeeming the Enlightenment', p. 607.
15. Ham, *The Lie*.
16. See 'Life on Venus? We're still looking'. 'We're working on getting more data that will tell us if phosphine is there, and where and how variable it is,' as Clara Sousa-Silva, one of the team who made the discovery, puts it (ibid., p. 24); phosphine is a gas that, as far as is known, can only come from living organisms.
17. See Beall, 'The Milky Way could be home to 5 billion planets like Earth'. Being Earth-like does not guarantee the existence of life of course, but it is an intriguing finding nevertheless.

Chapter 5

Dissent in the Sciences

Like religion, science has been prone to dogmatism historically, with bitter disputes taking place when established theories were challenged by dissenting voices. Since in most cases those theories had formed the basis of traditional knowledge about the world for centuries, it was no small matter to claim that they might be wrong. This is the landscape that Thomas S. Kuhn's work in the philosophy and history of science was concerned with, where scientific 'paradigms', as he dubbed them, have defined how the subject was to be viewed and taught, as well as what it was and was not acceptable to call into question about its theories and methods.[1] Every great change in physics, for example, has led to heated exchanges between defenders of the existing paradigm and those propounding a new theory, which generally has involved adopting a radically different worldview incompatible with the old – the difference, as was the case with the clash of Ptolemaic and Copernican astronomy, between the Sun orbiting the Earth or the Earth the Sun. Whichever one you believed in, you had to reject the claims of the other, the difference was that stark. Eventually the Copernican system became the accepted paradigm, registering a clear victory for dissent in the process.[2] But scientific enquiry has continued to identify contradictions and anomalies in even the best-established theories over the years, leading to a regular series of disputes between the profession's gatekeepers, who rarely give up without a fight, and those espousing newly incompatible theories and concepts – paradigm wars, as it were, which more often than not become clashes between the older and younger generation of scientists. Once the older generation has gone, the entire process starts all over again with an emerging new one. (Kuhn's conception of scientific history has been criticised as being rather too neat, but in broad general terms it still provides a useful overview of how the scientific community reacts to new theories.[3])

So sweeping have the changes proved to be in modern physics, however, that science as a whole has become less dogmatically inclined than heretofore, although it can still happen, as revealed by all the controversy over the search for a grand unified theory reconciling Einsteinian physics with quantum mechanics. Sharp exchanges between the respective sides are by no means unknown in the field's professional publications and the theories do contradict each other, and quite dramatically too, at several points (what works at the macro level does not always at the micro – and vice-versa, and no-one has as yet managed to bridge the gap to the satisfaction of both sides in the dispute, despite intensive work on a series of intriguing new theories such as loop quantum gravity[4]). Nevertheless, the need for constant challenge to existing theories has become accepted in science and the value of dissent as a permanent factor in its practices well recognised; one of the most critical scientific values, as a *New Scientist* editorial has put it, is 'organised scepticism'.[5] Paradigms, such as they are, have become more flexible than they used to be, which holds a useful lesson for our political life, where uncritical belief still plays far too large a part. (The notion that because your political hero says it, then it must be true, is a staple attitude on the far right – just think of President Trump's followers. It is one that dissent is having real difficulty grappling with.) There needs to be a great deal more provisionality about belief in general, a willingness to be, as Jean-François Lyotard put it, 'svelte' in our thinking, always adaptable to changing circumstances such that dogmatism is avoided, reacting instead with 'flexibility, speed, metamorphic capacity'.[6] That would constitute an organised scepticism for our daily lives, a trait I will expand on in Chapter 7. Conspiracy theory, as we have noted, has no time for provisionality and signally lacks the characteristics of svelteness, especially when it comes to dissenting views, which are simply dismissed as part of the conspiracy. As the physicist Jim Al-Khalili has put it, conspiracists ought to be considered 'the polar opposite' to scientists, in that they do not entertain doubts, taking their theory to be sacrosanct.[7] That is, unfortunately enough, all too often the case with politicians as well, who are notoriously reluctant to admit either mistakes or changes of mind. If that ever does happen, critics are invariably swift to dub it a U-turn, which in politics as currently practised is taken to denote a policy failure and thus incompetence on the part of the government, immediately generating lots of bad publicity in the media and usually a fall in the government's approval ratings. Scientists, however, have to be far more sanguine about the periodic need for such manoeuvres, all the more so when it is becoming increasingly apparent that reality itself may lie beyond our ability to describe, or measure, with the precision that science has traditionally sought and the general public have come to expect, perhaps being instead a 'fuzzy' phenomenon (a point I will be picking up on later in the chapter).[8]

Theory, method and testing

The search for a grand unified theory to complete the 'standard model' has given rise to some serious problems for physicists, as some of the theories being used to fill in gaps in the model go beyond any test yet devised. They appear to work, but their validity cannot be proved (or, increasingly, even measured). String theory is one of the main culprits here, being a theory which appears to clear up some critical problems in the standard model, but cannot as such be tested experimentally. On the one hand it is considered to be a successful theory, making sense of phenomena no other extant theory seems able to, but on the other it has not to date satisfied the primary requirement of the modern scientific method: a critical experiment proving its claims. While it still has its committed adherents, who repeatedly point up how well it functions in theoretical terms and the problems that it resolves, it is beginning to lose the support of many others in the field because of its failure to yield experimental results. Unless that crucial test is forthcoming soon, then it is unlikely to retain much credibility within the profession and science will revert to its default mode of putting forward other theories, as is already happening in this area. Scientists become very restless in such situations, keen to probe other possibilities when they run up against a barrier; scientific history is full of theories which have fallen by the wayside. Even the standard model itself is under threat from such a fate, with many physicists starting to suspect, however reluctantly, that it may no longer be fit for purpose and might need to be entirely replaced, although no-one is quite sure how, or as yet with what. '[T]here is something seriously wrong with our understanding of the cosmos', Stuart Clark notes in *New Scientist*, because 'everything is speeding apart more quickly than we expect'.[9] This raises the rather disorienting possibility that '[o]ur best model of the cosmos, a seemingly serenely sailing ship, might be holed beneath the water line'.[10] Another Copernican-style paradigm shift may be awaiting us: not so much a case of 'watch this space' as 'watch this space-time'.

There are several other theories in modern physics that seem stubbornly resistant to experimental confirmation. No theory of dark matter has so far been conclusively proved, for example (and there are quite a few of them vying for our attention, all sounding more than somewhat strange to the layperson). Dark energy is in the same position, being if anything an even more bewildering phenomenon: 'a mysterious addition to the standard model of cosmology that continues to evade characterisation', as Clark has to admit on behalf of the scientific profession.[11] Since dark energy is estimated to form around 68 per cent of the mass of the universe (dark matter constituting another 27 per cent or so) this leaves a very considerable gap in our knowledge of the universe and how it works. Visible matter counts as only 5 per cent, a negligible amount in terms of trying to explain the physics of the entire universe. Then there is a large array of particles and antiparticles whose existence is at best notional, with new ones constantly being posited (such as the purely hypothetical axions for dark matter). Supersymmetry theorises an antiparticle for every particle and while it has its strong advocates, it divides opinion also. Many physicists are left unconvinced by this theory, although it is an area of considerable interest in terms of explaining what happened in the early days of the universe after the Big Bang, leaving a universe dominated by matter rather than antimatter. Since the principle is that '[t]he two annihilate when they meet' there should be no imbalance at all and thus no matter left in the universe; but as there patently is, there are various speculative theories doing the rounds in particle physics as to how this apparently unlikely outcome might be explained.[12] (The Big Bang itself remains a topic of controversy as to its nature and cause as well, being an event that transcends human understanding.) Scientists put forward such theories to fill in the gaps in the standard model, so it can qualify as an example of system-building, but experimental proof is always necessary to back it up. If such proof does not materialise within a reasonable length of time, then doubt will set in and scientists will start exploring other possible ways of explaining the phenomena causing the problem (the 'science' of Marxism, tellingly, forbids such a move). The particle physicist Edward Blucher has neatly summed up the current situation with regard to matter and antimatter: 'Studying the universe is like building a building, so you have to understand and measure every brick . . . If, in the end, this is not enough to produce matter–antimatter asymmetry, fine – it is still an important brick.'[13]

Science is a very dynamic activity, therefore, and doubt plays a very critical role in that process. Theories come and go but are always under pressure to justify themselves, otherwise dissenters will soon make their scepticism known: every 'brick' has to be accounted for or else credibility begins to wane. Svelteness is built into the modern scientific method, where change and provisionality have to be accepted as the normal state of affairs. When necessary, beliefs must be shed and there should be no sense of failure about having to do this, even if it means ditching theories such as the standard model. Finding out what does not work is just as useful as finding out what does, frustrating though this must be to scientists who have expended significant time and effort on an eventually discarded theory or line of enquiry (even more frustrating than some of them would want to admit publicly, one suspects, but the principle is accepted throughout the profession nevertheless).

Svelte politics, however, is not much in evidence as one looks around the scene at present, although it is needed there just as much as it is in the scientific world. That is partly our own fault, however, as we seem to be notably less forgiving of politicians changing their mind than of ourselves doing so. It is that U-turn reaction mentioned above, which the average politician dreads when in office and will do just about anything to avoid; trying to lay the blame on others if ever forced into this by events is a fairly routine, but never very convincing, response.

Science and politics

The relationship between science and politics is not always a harmonious one; we have already seen how science and religion have often been at loggerheads in the past, and still are today in terms of creationism (a textbook example of dogmatism and its distorting, 'fake dissent', qualities in action). At least in principle, most modern governments defer to scientific knowledge (with certain worrying exceptions I shall go on to consider below), as was very apparent in the coronavirus pandemic, when government ministers in the UK and elsewhere kept insisting that their policies for dealing with it were all based on what scientists were telling them. Scientists were even included in governmental press briefings outlining the progress of the handling of the disease, with technical questions being passed on to them by ministers for expert answers. The clear impression being communicated was that politics was being led by science, which became something of a mantra for the political class. While there were significant exceptions to this reliance on scientific expertise – Donald Trump did not always stay on message (to the obvious dismay of his public health officials) and President Bolsonaro of Brazil flatly refused to believe any of the evidence – most nations closely followed the scientific advice about how best to cope with the outbreak. In the main, politicians were relieved to let science carry the burden of responsibility for the difficult decisions having to be made over such issues as quarantining. (A more cynical interpretation, however, would be that it was a case of politicians trying to shift responsibilities on to others and away from themselves, which is how it often came across in the UK, where there was considerable unease in the scientific community about how they were being used by the government, often to cover up its deficiencies. Being led by the science often turned into blaming the science for anything that went wrong in the implementation of government decisions, and there was no lack of this as the pandemic ground on. Scientists and government were often out of step on the issue of quarantining as well, which created a fair amount of tension in the relationship.)

When it comes to other issues such as climate change, governments are not always as ready to rely on scientists' findings or to follow their recommendations. Scientists internationally are all but unanimous in their belief in climate change – or crisis, or emergency, as you will – and have emphasised as strongly as they can (through organisations such as the UN's Intergovernmental Panel on Climate Change (IPCC)) the need to reduce carbon emissions drastically, and quickly, to ward off environmental disaster. Even politicians who accept these findings have been slow to react, however, and, more to the point, there are many who do not accept them at all, making it very difficult to put together meaningful global action to meet the required targets. Brazil has massively expanded its clearing operations in the Amazonian rain forest, reducing the efficiency of one of the most important areas for carbon absorption on the planet (its 'lungs' as they been called), which will render the targets even more difficult to meet; all in the cause of boosting the economy, the fallback position for all too many political leaders, all too many times. America under the Trump presidency withdrew from the relevant international agreements on carbon reduction and although the Biden administration has reversed that decision, valuable time has been lost in dealing with the problem. It has to be said that opting in or out on presidential whim hardly seems a viable way of approaching the topic; all it demonstrates is how politics can get in the way of pursuing solutions. America continues to be committed to a fossil-fuel-based economy (oil production being a significant sector of its economy), as, to be fair, are many other national governments, either implicitly or explicitly.

For all their public pronouncements about supporting climate change agreements, most politicians are reluctant to take any steps that adversely affect their nation's economy: growth continues to be their main aim and that inevitably means more, rather than less, carbon emissions – a connection politicians rarely bother to mention when claiming the credit for an improving economy, which is generally considered to be an election-winner. Politics is therefore allowed to take precedence over science on this issue, despite the very obvious risks involved. Scientific dissent about this policy is either dismissed or simply ignored by most of the political class, but it has to keep making its case as forcefully as possible, particularly as the scientific projections continue to get more worrying – as they clearly do (one in June 2020 was described as 'incredibly alarming' by a UK Met Office spokesperson, but governments are skilled at letting such comments pass them by). Betting that scientists are either mistaken in their alarm, or that they are conspiring together to generate greater funding for their pet projects (as some climate change sceptics have claimed, with little corroborating evidence, it has to be noted) is taking a considerable risk with our collective future. In this area anyway, there is a glaringly obvious disconnect between science and politics and it is clearly the economy that is the sticking point. Even 'incredibly alarming' data on rising global temperatures will not be enough to stop most politicians (with an eye to re-election) from focusing more on the economy than the environment. It is turning into one of the most intractable disputes of our time, and one that looks likely to haunt the next few generations. Unfortunately, power lies overwhelmingly on the economy's side; even the current pandemic has not altered that, with economic considerations often seeming to be dictating the character of governmental responses in, as notable cases in point, the UK, the US and Brazil.

As long as the economy dominates in that fashion, with governments giving precedence to its needs, then the environment will continue to be a critical area for dissent, giving rise to movements such as Extinction Rebellion (also, sadly, to the reality denial of the QAnon movement). It is yet another area where the limits of democracy become very apparent, prompting animated protest that is very much a case of telling those in authority what they do not want to hear (such protests inevitably have become yet another 'law and order' issue to the authorities when they take to the streets, with the right-wing media falling into line over this interpretation). No matter how much climate change is denied, or ignored, by politicians and the corporate sector, however, its effects are becoming ever more obvious to the wider public through the increasing incidence of extreme weather events – presumably regarded as just so much fake news by the QAnon community. Record heatwaves, rainfalls, droughts and storms are part of our everyday experience nowadays and the forecasts are that they will become progressively more extreme unless there is a very significant change in lifestyles globally. The rise of Extinction Rebellion (XR) signals a loss of faith in the ability of our system as currently constituted to deal with this problem, a frustration that liberal democracy remains so transfixed by the phenomenon of economic growth that it cannot admit the danger this poses for humankind and set about reining it in significantly. XR is dismissed as a mere nuisance by most politicians, but ignoring their complaints or banning their public protests will not make climate change, or the tipping points this is predicted to generate sooner rather than later, go away (in just a few decades with the North Atlantic Gulf Stream, which might then close down alto-gether, yet another highly alarming prospect). Nor will it lessen the appeal of groups like QAnon.

The commitment to economic growth seems all but hard-wired into liberal democracy, an integral part of its development and what sets it apart from other socio-political systems, enabling it to claim that it reliably delivers a higher standard of living (com-munism may have had the same commitment, but never anything like the same success in its delivery). Neither is science immune from this ethos; it is, after all, the source of the ideas for the tech-nology that is so instrumental in driving this growth. Science and politics have a very complex relationship, therefore, especially when we remember that without political funding, as well as funding from the corporate sector to develop its technology to sell on to consumers in an ever-evolving array of new products, science as the major undertaking we know it today would barely exist. Liberal democracy has politicised science (as communism did too in its own way, putting it completely at the service of the party ideology) and movements like XR make us all uncomfortably aware of this, of how politicians pick and choose what they want from scientific research in order to score ideological points. The politicisation of science is something that dissenters should always be aware of and be prepared to bring to public attention as a topic for debate. Scepticism about the role of politicians in this area is entirely justified, especially since a significant amount of scientific research is directed towards developing weapons for military use, something that scientists themselves are often very conflicted by. Again, it is the economic benefits of this that governments invariably emphasise; arms sales is an area that always seems to remain buoyant – unfortunately enough.

No modern political system has politicised science more than the Soviet regime, which especially in its early stages (and most notably under Stalin) sought to use it as a way of proving the validity of Marx's theories. Marx had claimed that he was putting forward a 'science of society' that was the answer to all social and political problems, and the physical sciences were thereafter to be judged in relation to that. Friedrich Engels provided an early example of the link that Marxist theoreticians were looking for between physical processes (in this case biology) and their science of society, with his discussion of the Hegelian concept of the negation of the negation. The development from a seed to a plant was taken by Engels to be a natural demonstration of the Hegelian dialectic, in that each stage of the process involved a negation of the last to form a new entity: thesis to antithesis to synthesis. For Engels, this was a 'very simple process that is taking place everywhere and every day', as with a grain of barley:

> if such a grain of barley meets with conditions which are normal for it, if it falls on suitable soil then under the influence of heat and moisture a specific change occurs in it, it germinates; the grain as such ceases to exist, it is negated, and in its place there appears the plant which has arisen from it, the negation of the grain.[14]

The plant in its turn produces seeds, starting the process all over again, just as the Hegelian dialectic's sequence does, which to Engels is further proof of the intrinsically dialectical nature of reality. To question either the Hegelian dialectic or Marx's appropriation of it is made to appear to be denying the facts of the physical world, which are taken to validate Marxist principles such as class struggle being a basic feature of social existence throughout history. Dialectics becomes a universal law, a science in the political world no less than in nature, with the consequence that dissenting from Marxist theory becomes all but impossible for communists. The overriding concern of scientific research under communism is to find evidence supporting Marxism, suppressing whatever contradicts it. Scientific method is expected to conform to the principles of dialectical materialism.

A negation of a negation may be an interesting (even somewhat poetic) way of describing the life cycle of a plant, but it hardly proves that dialectics is a science as the term is commonly understood. The logic or otherwise of the argument is less important, however, than the mind-set that it reveals, whereby the theory's truth is assumed to be beyond doubt and its universality self-evident. Marxist theory was to be treated as the basis of scientific research, and if the two ever came into contradiction then it was the research that must be at fault rather than Marxism. That attitude completely undermines the notion that Marxism is a science, however, since science depends on constant testing of its beliefs and a commitment to their provisionality; they hold until something with greater predictive accuracy comes along (as it almost always will in time). Dissenting views are an integral part of the scientific ethos, not a cause for suppression by its authority figures if they raise doubts about conventionally approved theories. It is fair to say that without dissent any belief system declines into a mere faith, where the only thing that is being tested is the depth of the individual's loyalty to the relevant beliefs (just as in the religious sphere with figures like John Bunyan). The politicisation of science is effectively a doomed enterprise, showing up the weakness of the politicisers' case as much as anything.

This overt politicisation came to a head with communism in notorious cases such as that involving the work of the Soviet biologist Trofim Lysenko during Stalin's reign. With the science of society behind them, the Soviet hierarchy was convinced that its implementation would inevitably lead to a far more efficient and progressive socio-political system that would outstrip capitalism in its production, both industrially and agriculturally. The political imperative was to work out ways of doing so, or at least to make it appear that this had been done. It was an invitation, in other words, to indulge in some very creative policy-based evidence-making, which Lysenko duly came up with in terms of improving agricultural production, claiming that his findings were compatible with dialectical materialism (that being the essential requirement). Lysenko rejected standard genetic theories and his ideas were taken seriously enough by Stalin and the party leadership to trigger a purge of the work of any biologists who disagreed with Lysenkoism, many of whom were subsequently imprisoned. Lysenko's theories proved false and the entire episode constituted a very significant setback for the development of this field (with many other areas of scientific practice in the Soviet Union undergoing a similar fate if they were judged to be ideologically unsound), as is only too likely to be the case where the science is made to fit the politics. (It is worth noting, however, that despite such political repression, later generations of Soviet scientists, notably the physicist Andrei Sakharov, were nevertheless prepared to train their research-honed analytical skills on the regime's human rights record, turning themselves into dissidents in the regime's eyes.[15])

Although the process is not as sinister as prevailed in the Soviet Union, science is nevertheless subject to a considerable degree of politicisation in the liberal democratic world too, its practitioners regularly finding themselves expected to meet targets set by their funding source, whether that is governmental or commercial. It is a situation that can represent a worrying threat to upholding the discipline's ideals, as is made plain in Stuart Ritchie's book *Science Fictions: Exposing Fraud, Bias, Negligence and Hype in Science*. The problem Ritchie points out is the constant pressure that scientists are under to publish and to hype their research as much as possible, with the aim of winning more funding grants and enhancing their reputation (and thus promotion prospects); that is the way the university system internationally operates these days and no academic scientist is immune to this. Such an approach, with its tendency to making exaggerated and often unsubstantiable claims in order to draw attention to one's work at the expense of one's competitors, very obviously cuts against the 'organised scepticism' and dispassionately analytical methods on which science depends so heavily for its credibility, something that the race to find a vaccine to treat Covid-19 has brought sharply into focus. Epidemics, and more especially pandemics, are always good for the pharmaceutical business. Once a successful vaccine is discovered, it is marketed globally and becomes a source of very considerable profits to whatever pharmaceutical company holds the rights, and companies are not necessarily going to be all that patient in waiting for trials to be done and results to be methodically investigated – in a pandemic particularly, with politicians queuing up to be the first to gain access to the treatment and offering considerable inducements to obtain that right (as President Trump lost no time in doing, for example). Science is in that sense tied into the market economy, a situation that has at least the potential to lead to compromise in terms of its ideals. The lure of profit can always distort idealism, as can the desire to appear ahead of the field in a university system increasingly under pressure to prove its value to governments and other funding bodies (value which is increasingly being defined as financial, and not just in the scientific subjects; humanities academics have to wrestle with this expectation as well). Despite this, scientists themselves still realise what those ideals are and will be able to recognise where corners are being cut and claims are suspect. Critics like Ritchie will continue to come forward as long as there are controversies around replication of scientific experiments or studies, which is where anything less than stringent application of scientific method in the original becomes most obvious. As Ritchie sums it up: 'If it won't replicate, then it's hard to describe what you've done as scientific at all' (the fate of the MMR–autism link referred to in Chapter 1).[16] No matter how much hype, bias and dogmatism may try to bypass that test, scientists in general will know that replication is a requirement that must be met eventually, and consistently; dissent within the profession over any such failure cannot so easily be erased, no matter how much politicians and the corporate sector may try to cover it up for their own devious reasons. The whole area, however, is something of an ethical minefield for all the parties involved, and is likely to remain so as long as political expediency and the profit motive are playing such central roles. Dissent will regularly find itself coming into conflict with the profit motive.

Science, certainty and reality

What politicians would like from science is information that enables them to say things with certainty and that in turn reinforces their belief in their ideology – a position that to their mind puts them one step ahead of any dissenting views that might be expressed. Science provides the aura of credibility that they can exploit to their advantage with the general public, implying that they have something objective to fall back on, that it is not just their opinion that lies behind their policies. It is unlikely, however, that the average politician keeps especially up to date on the philosophical questions that are arising about the aims, and more importantly the limits, of scientific method. If they did, it should make them pause about thinking they can rely so confidently on 'the science' to back up their assumption of authority. Scientists themselves are well aware of the limits of scientific method and of the likelihood that any of their theories – including the frustratingly elusive grand unified theory – will eventually meet limits to what it can either describe or know with certainty. It is a case not just of lacking the tools to probe into the nature of reality (a point made by John D. Barrow in his book *Impossibility*[17]), but of reality itself not being as clear-cut and knowable as we would like to think. To some scientists, reality instead appears to be characterised by a fuzziness that makes descriptions of it, as well as knowledge of it, always less than precise. Indeed, imprecision seems to be built into the nature of reality, hence into our perception of it; we live, as Eddy Keming Chen puts it, in a 'fuzzy-verse', where '[m]athematics . . . may never completely capture the objective order of the universe'.[18] As a case in point, percentages can be attached to both dark matter and dark energy (95 per cent in total of the matter in the universe, as we have seen), but that can hardly be said to 'capture' that objective order.

Whether it is possible to capture the objective order comprehensively has taxed philosophers as well as scientists down the years. Immanuel Kant's concept of things-in-themselves posits a limit to human knowledge about reality, as they lie in a realm beyond human perception, the noumenal as opposed to the phenomenal one of our everyday experience.[19] Kant's conception of reality has come under attack from a recent philosophical movement called speculative realism. The argument there is that we really can experience objective reality and that it is not hidden from us as Kant claims.[20] Whether that means we can get past the fuzziness posited by Chen is more debatable, as that implies we could never put together an entirely accurate picture of the objective order of the universe.

Vagueness, particularly about measurement and thus the descriptions following on from that, may just have to be accepted as an inescapable element of both reality and human perception of it, an uncomfortable conclusion to contemplate for all those expecting certainty to be forthcoming from science.[21] Politicians who would be content for their ideology or policies to be thought of as fuzzy would be few and far between (just imagine the likes of Trump or the Brexiteers even contemplating such a possibility). Add in the unknowability that Barrow sees as yet another inescapable part of the scientific enterprise and assumptions of authority, or claims to be in total control, based on science begin to look seriously misguided. There are, as Barrow warns us, 'limits and barriers which cannot be crossed', even for scientists.[22] No matter how much researchers might succeed in pushing the current set of limits back, limits will always exist (explaining *why*, rather than *how*, the Big Bang happened could be the ultimate limit; except to the religious of course, who can always assign the event to God). It could well be that a final grand unified theory is an unrealistic ambition, although that will not deter the scientific temperament from striving to get ever closer to it. As long as humanity is around there is unlikely to be an end of science (an end of human history is, however, another matter entirely, especially if the scientific recommendations on climate change go unheeded).

If you are seeking certainty, therefore, science is not the place to go looking for it, not with provisionality and fuzziness as embedded features. Both politicians and the general public need to bear that very firmly in mind when assessing the implementation of policies; there is no magic wand that will guarantee the success of such endeavours and dissenters must keep pointing this out to those in power, in times of pandemic or otherwise. This is not an argument against science, which goes on generating more and more useful knowledge despite its limits, as well as more about our misconceptions as to its capabilities. As Carlo Rovelli has insisted, 'it is reliability that we need, not certainty' for our theories, and 'science *is* the search for the most credible answers available, not for answers pretending to certainty'.[23] Opting for reliability rather than pretending to certainty would improve our politics no less than our science, because there are just too many variables concerned with politics to make such pretensions at all realistic: something to bear in mind the next time an election rolls around and candidates start making claims as to what they are confident they could deliver if in office. A trade deal with America to make up for any losses the UK might suffer from Brexit (a key component of the Leave strategy) assumed that President Trump, a keen supporter of the idea, would be re-elected in 2020; his defeat has left that plan in limbo as the new administration of President Biden has announced it does not consider it a priority. The curse of the political variable strikes again. Whether those involved care to admit it or not, there is an inherent fuzziness about any projection made of the political future; it depends on events, and those, as Lyotard points out, can always catch us by surprise.

Conclusion: the scepticism of science

Science thrives on continual, 'organised', scepticism about its theories, therefore, and dissenting views are welcomed by the scientific community as a sign that its members are doing their job properly, rigorously testing the discipline's theories to determine their ongoing validity and keeping an especially watchful eye out for proof of replication (as well as acknowledging all the attendant fuzziness that will accompany this). It is science's own version of democracy's 'perpetual contest'. Dogmatic attitudes can still creep in, especially when any large-scale paradigm shift looms up, or when political and commercial pressures to deliver results as quickly as possible intensify, but by and large science is an area that recognises its crucial dependence on dissent: science would not be science without it, although when science interacts with politics the situation becomes considerably more complicated. Politicians are prone to use science if it helps their cause, but equally to ignore it, or even question its competence, if it does not. They will defer to it only if it seems to provide them with an ideological advantage, and science can give no guarantee that this condition will last: there is only so far you can go with Lysenkoism, as a salutary case in point. Fuzzy universes pose even more of a problem, given that wrestling with metaphysics is not a political speciality. While political and commercial pressure may cause some scientists to make unwarranted claims for their research (every profession has its careerists and those prepared to cut corners to gain an advantage over their rivals), the reality of what it subsequently delivers will serve to undermine these – as sceptics will always be quick off the mark to draw to our attention. More than anything else science ought to give us a sense of proportion as to the extent and the nature of our knowledge and what we can assume from it, a particularly valuable lesson in the face of ideology's pretensions. If even the standard model can be thrown into doubt, then what else could not be?

Notes

1. See Kuhn, *The Structure of Scientific Revolutions*.
2. See Kuhn, *The Copernican Revolution*.
3. For a critique of Kuhn's theories, see the various contributions to Lakatos and Musgrave, *Criticism and the Growth of Knowledge*.
4. Carlo Rovelli, for example, is a strong proponent of loop quantum gravity, arguing that '[i]t is not the only direction explored in the search for a quantum theory of gravity, but it is the one I consider the most promising' (Rovelli, *Reality Is Not What It Seems*, p. 137).
5. 'All that glitters. . .'.

6. Lyotard, 'A Svelte Appendix to the Postmodern Question', p. 28.
7. Al-Khalili, 'Doubt is essential for science'.
8. See, for example, Chen, 'Welcome to the fuzzy-verse'.
9. Clark, 'A quantum twist in space-time', p. 34.
10. Ibid.
11. Clark, 'Measuring up the universe', p. 35.
12. Crane, 'Why matter exists at all'.
13. Quoted ibid. Crane suggests that proof for one of the theories, that neutrinos are responsible for the imbalance, 'will probably be found by experiments being worked on now, like the T2HK experiment in Japan or DUNE in the US' (ibid.), but the requirements of scientific method weigh heavily on that 'probably'.
14. Engels, *Anti-Dühring*, pp. 172–3.
15. On this, see Bernstein, 'Science and Dissent'.
16. Ritchie, *Science Fictions*, p. 5.
17. For Barrow, '[c]omplete knowledge is a tempting pie in the sky', hardly a phrase the authoritarian-minded would want to endorse (Barrow, *Impossibility*, p. 3).
18. Chen, 'Welcome to the fuzzy-verse', p. 40.
19. See Kant, *Critique of Pure Reason*.
20. For a survey of the various positions within speculative realism, see Kleinherenbrink, 'New Images of Thought'.
21. Benoit Mandelbrot had earlier pointed out how we could never accurately measure such things as coastlines, because the fractal nature of physical reality meant there would always be self-similar patterns within the patterns being measured, precluding any final measurement (see Mandelbrot, *The Fractal Geometry of Nature*). Impossibility yet again intrudes on the search for complete knowledge, even in such an apparently restricted domain; physics shades into metaphysics at such points as the objective order yet again evades capture.
22. Barrow, *Impossibility*, p. 1.
23. Rovelli, *Reality Is Not What It Seems*, p. 231.

Chapter 6

Aesthetic Dissent

Although the arts would appear to be an area that allows freedom of expression to participants and that has no overall authority dictating what individuals can or cannot do, it is surprising how set in its ways and resistant to change it can become at the professional and institutional level. While amateurs are more or less free to do what they want, things change when one moves on to that other level. There, styles and methods can take on an air of authority that can be very restrictive to those with unconventional ideas, as often happened in traditional arts teaching, with certain styles being considered to stand as models. Modernism in its early phase represented a concerted rejection of aesthetic authority, challenging preconceptions and breaking conventions across all the arts and the traditions that they represented, but it soon became restrictive in its turn, laying down principles of what could count as meaningful artistic practice through its control over many of the artworld's key institutions; either you followed the modernist line or you were damned as reactionary by its leading figures and your work denigrated. While postmodernism represented a rejection of the modernist creed and its obsession with originality, it too came to be a restrictive aesthetic in time, judging all artistic activity according to its own fairly rigid set of principles. Each style had a method that it deemed to be authoritative, leading it to be critical of work which did not conform to this. In effect, dissent was yet again being outlawed; there was a new grand narrative and to diverge from it was to take a risk with your professional reputation. Popularity with the public would not be enough to change the minds of your peers either; in fact, many modernists viewed popularity with something like disdain, as if it meant there was a lack of seriousness in the work of anyone who achieved such acclaim. It was as if artworks had to be difficult to understand to qualify as authentic. Postmodernists may have made far more of an effort to win public favour, but they had their own notions of what constituted authenticity and these could be just as exclusive in their way.

Modernism and the rejection of tradition

Modernism involved a very self-conscious rejection of tradition, emphasising originality above all, particularly originality of form. In consequence, painting moved away from realism to abstraction; music embraced dissonance; fictional writing dispensed with linear narrative, and even with the rules of standard grammar in some cases (the 'stream of consciousness' mode encouraging this); architecture dropped ornamentation in favour of geometrical severity of line. Even though the general public proved in the main highly resistant to such experimentation, creative artists nevertheless continued on with it, claiming that it was the public's own fault if they failed to understand or appreciate the new style and that it was the artist's duty to challenge the audience's preconceptions – and not to let up doing so. Contemporaries who did not follow what amounted to the party line found themselves being publicly mocked.

In music, composers in the late romantic style – Sergei Rachmaninov being a notable case in point – had to endure such mockery from their peers who had espoused the twelve-tone system, which they claimed to be the only possible future for musical composition (despite history strongly suggesting that one is always a hostage to fortune to make such a claim). Critics such as the influential Theodor W. Adorno were to endorse that view, arguing that the work of the founder of the twelve-tone style (now usually referred to as serialism), Arnold Schoenberg, represented an irreversible break with music's past, revolutionising it to the extent that there was no way back from this:

> All the tonal combinations employed in the past by no means stand indiscriminately at the disposal of the composer today . . . It is not simply that these sounds are antiquated and untimely, but that they are false. They no longer fulfill their function.[1]

Igor Stravinsky, for instance, who in the 1920s was using just such older 'tonal combinations' in his neoclassical style, having been praised as a daring modernist for earlier works like *The Rite of Spring* (1913), was to Adorno guilty of 'a retrogression into the traditional' that signalled the 'decline' of the modernist ideal.[2] Drawing on Marxist theory, Adorno argues that composers who follow the Stravinsky line suffer from 'false musical consciousness'.[3] That would mean that a significant number of Stravinsky's contemporaries whose music features very prominently in concert programming in our own time (Rachmaninov and Jean Sibelius being outstanding examples) should all be written off, their works to be considered full of 'impotent cliches' that have nothing to say to the modern listener.[4] Even more provocatively, it should mean that all the audiences listening to these composers now are similarly afflicted with the wrong kind of consciousness, taking refuge in the safe and conventional instead of challenging themselves.

In this context it is also worth remembering that Johann Sebastian Bach's musical style was considered to be old-fashioned for the latter part of his career, not up to date with the rococo style that was then becoming the vogue. He was more appreciated as an organist than a composer during his life and his sons Carl Philipp Emanuel and Johann Christian had a higher reputation as composers in the later eighteenth century than their father did (Carl Philipp Emanuel has been undergoing something of a revival of late, but nothing on the scale of his father). False musical consciousness in Bach perhaps (it would be a brave commentator who would argue that nowadays)? Or is the cult of the new more problematic than modernist theorists would be prepared to admit?

One factor that does work against such assessments is time: Bach's music is from so far in back the past, and so many styles have come and gone since then, that it can be judged on its own merits alone without having to be compared stylistically to the work of his contemporaries (none of whom have attained anything like Bach's level of reputation). The same can now be said about Rachmaninov and Sibelius and other non-modernist composers of their generation: what their modernist composer peers thought of them back in the early twentieth century no longer seems all that relevant – certainly not to the general public anyway, who happily turn up in large numbers at concert halls to hear their music, which is now a staple of the classical repertoire internationally. Time enables us to have a very different perspective on a composer's place in musical history, one less dependent on whether they were considered to be avant-garde or not in their generation: novelty wears off eventually and is not always what the audience is looking for anyway (nor should it be expected to). I am no particular fan of Rachmaninov myself, but that is because I find most of his music overly sentimental, not because it does not use the twelve-tone system. Schoenberg's music still finds an audience, if far less so than that of Rachmaninov or Sibelius, but it is appreciated more for its dramatic (even melodramatic) quality than because of its use of serial technique. Serialism was an interesting experiment and one that musical trends had been working up to in the work of various composers from at least Richard Wagner onwards, but it was by no means a blueprint for the future of composition. In a sense it was being authoritarian ever to claim that it was: laws of taste are notoriously difficult to lay down and Adorno's based on Schoenbergian serialism clearly have not stood the test of time.

There was nothing wrong with the rationale behind modernism – finding new means of expression is something that creative artists have always been interested in and no doubt will continue to be – but there was in its assumption that it was now the only legitimate way to engage in the arts – or to judge artworks. Elements of the past are always around in the present and it would in fact be very disorienting for most of us if they were not. Iconoclasm for its own sake can become very wearing and modernist polemic can now seem just rather narrow-minded – as well as more than somewhat bullying, as no doubt non-modernists felt it to be during modernism's heyday (being told you are reactionary, or that your work is cliched, rarely goes down all that well). Admittedly, too much reverence for tradition can hinder creative expression, but its value in giving us a sense of context should not be underestimated. Rather ironically for a movement which started out with such revolutionary intentions, its rejection of tradition meant that modernism was to become distinctly authoritarian in attitude, judging all artistic production according to its own creed (just as traditionalists had done in the past), always on the lookout for retrogressions to dismiss as misguided and lacking in artistic integrity. In Adorno's view, you had to choose Schoenberg over Stravinsky because that was where progress lay and modernism prided itself in being in the vanguard of this movement. In order to keep progressing and creating a new kind of culture, new methods of artistic expression had to be discovered. Modernists like Adorno just did not believe that it was possible to use older models after such huge changes in society as the twentieth century had seen. Those models were considered to be tainted by association with the culture that developed them; continuing to follow them was to be avoided at all costs if one wanted to be considered a serious creative artist or thinker. (Just as a side note, Stravinsky did experiment with serial technique in the latter stages of his career, as in the ballet score *Agon* (1957), but by then the controversy over it had died down somewhat. Serialism had become just one of the many options open to a composer instead of a test of one's artistic, and for Adorno also ideological, integrity. By that time as well, electronic music was being touted as the future, but that has not proved to be the case either.) Assessing aesthetic value on the basis of an either/or choice of styles is, however, a very reductive way of looking at the arts. It was just as reductive under the regime of socialist realism in the Soviet bloc, which merely reversed the choice of styles, insisting that non-modernism was the only acceptable mode for Soviet artists to use. Authority is a law unto itself in such matters – and not a particularly reliable one.

Jazz is another area where stylistic change has led to bitter exchanges amongst both performers and their audiences. Modern jazz developed from the bebop movement in the 1940s onwards and it created a deep rift in the jazz world that echoes the one found in classical music with the arrival of twelve-tone composition: a sense of a discourse being turned on its head, to the consternation of the majority of its audience – and jazz, in the form of the big bands and the swing style, was highly popular at the time. Fans of modern jazz had a distinct tendency to look down on those who preferred older styles (I have to confess to being guilty of that attitude myself in my youth), claiming that to play in that way was a jazz equivalent of false consciousness. Modern jazz was, to such zealots, the only real jazz for artists to be playing from the advent of bebop onwards and they were particularly scathing of those who followed the trad jazz movement in the UK in the 1950s, which based itself on New Orleans jazz of the earlier twentieth century, recreating it as authentically as possible. For the modern jazz fan this was far too easy, reactionary rather than truly creative in the manner of the new idiom. When certain modern jazzmen – notably John Coltrane and Ornette Coleman – started to experiment in the 1960s with an atonal style reminiscent of twelve-tone ('free jazz' as Coleman's approach came to be called), then another rift occurred, with much the same accusations being traded across the new divide. The later development of jazz rock was also to prove alienating to many jazz fans, for whom it could never really qualify as true to the genre's ideals. False consciousness can crop up just about anywhere as far as zealotry goes and it is rarely of much use in assessing aesthetic value, which can never be that rigidly defined nor precise. No authority can dictate exactly what consciousness a creative artist should bring to his or her work; that has to remain an individual decision, which will then be subject to critical opinion on its merits.

Jazz fans have become far more respectful of the music's past and less critical of those musicians keeping the older styles alive in our own day (as classical musicians do in their field); but it is an object lesson as to how dissent can quickly turn into yet another grand narrative intolerant of any opposition to its assumed supremacy.

It is a tendency that keeps manifesting itself and that dissent should always be on the lookout for.

Postmodernism and the recasting of tradition

Postmodern dissent took an entirely different attitude towards tradition, recasting it to fit a new aesthetic paradigm based on dialogue between the old and the new. It was to be a case not of retrogression, therefore, but of reappropriation within a different cultural context; ostensibly a more generous attitude towards one's predecessors. Charles Jencks's work on architectural theory is crucial in this respect; his own theory of double coding provided a rationale for swerving away from the modernist paradigm and its obsession with originality and formal experimentation.[5] Double coding was a way of recreating a dialogue between artist and audience that had been largely lost under the modernist regime, when few, if any, concessions were being made to audience sensibilities: the 'shock of the new' was what was being sought at all times instead, and serial music and cubist art certainly delivered that (as did bebop and then free jazz). At worst, there was a 'take it or leave it' attitude towards much modernist creative production, with traditional values being deliberately rejected in favour of often extreme experimentation that alienated much of its potential audience; the pull of the past was definitely underestimated by modernists. Progress as the predominant social goal no longer had quite the same appeal by the latter stages of the twentieth century that it had for earlier cultural theorists such as Adorno (the lifestyle it involved was already beginning to be identified with the rapidly developing problem of climate change, for one thing); tradition was beginning to be seen in a more positive light and as worthy of reappraisal. Antagonism towards the past was now considered misplaced; postmodernists wanted to recycle it and show their ingenuity by what they managed to create through that exercise.

Jencks's pet hate was 'brutalism', the term usually attached to architecture's so-called International Style. This was austere in appearance, all straight lines and lack of colour or ornamentation, concrete and glass constituting the major construction materials: skyscrapers and tower blocks are its lasting legacy, and these can indeed be found in any of the world's countries (their major cities particularly). While brutalism could be defended on both social and aesthetic grounds, as almost any style can by its committed practitioners, it was its sheer ubiquity that was more problematic; its advocates became intensely dogmatic about it and brooked no criticism from the public. The International Style was a grand narrative which did not recognise the claims of other narratives: this was the way architecture was supposed to look and the public were just mistaken if they thought otherwise. It became the basis of architectural education, giving it a powerful hold over the profession's work. Jencks, on the other hand, was a fervent champion of colour and ornamentation, encouraging a style that the public could identify with rather than feel threatened by in the brutalist manner (his own work in the field of landscape art has been praised for its accessibility). Diversity was to be cultivated instead of uniformity. Pastiche became a dominant mode in postmodernism, therefore, with styles being mixed together playfully with little regard for notions of purity; originality was no longer the main point of the exercise, as artists sought to come to an accommodation with their audience, to entertain them rather than shock or confuse them. If references to modernism ever turned up in the pastiche they tended to be somewhat mocking in tone, as in the ad where a cubist-styled bottle of a well-known brand of mineral water was labelled 'Picasseau'. The alienating quality of so much modernism was to be studiously avoided; the audience was to be met half-way with familiar material, often laced with humour (rarely a modernist characteristic).

The attraction of experimentalism and originality did not die out, however, as the development of the theory of altermodernism was to prove. Altermodernism argued that the modernist ethos still had a place in the arts and that it was short-sighted to reject it altogether as postmodernists had done. The art theorist Nicolas Bourriaud claimed that postmodernism had become too predictable as a style, following a method which constrained artists to adopt certain procedures in order to attain professional approval.

It was time to reconsider our attitude towards modernism and rediscover what it offered to the creative imagination:

> Numerous contemporary artistic practices indicate . . . that we are on the verge of a leap, out of the postmodern period and the (essentialist) multicultural model from which it is indivisible, a leap that would give rise to a synthesis between modernism and post-colonialism. Let us then call this synthesis 'altermodernism'.[6]

Bourriaud's point is that both modernism in its original form and postmodernism had become too rule-bound, leading them to become judgemental about anything that did not fit their criteria. He wanted us to be much more open-minded about modernism and to recognise that it was still a valid way of expressing an artistic vision, that pastiche and irony had their limitations in terms of making us experience the world in new ways – as modernism most certainly did, even if it could take time for its value to become apparent as the shock of the new receded. It is just such opposition against orthodoxy, however defined, that I am arguing is necessary in all discourses, from politics and the sciences through to the arts. This was to be a modernism designed to co-exist with other styles: a compromise position compared to Adorno's rigidity. It is when criticism of a dominant theory is aggressively marginalised that problems develop and postmodernism could be as guilty of this in its way as modernism had been before it (if admittedly less strident and hectoring about it). There is no grand narrative in the arts, just a series of narratives which can be added to as the creative impulse takes you; peer pressure should not be dictating what the nature of those additions should be and it should be firmly resisted by the individual artist. The notion of there being a 'false' approach to artistic creation really does not stand up to much scrutiny; all that can be said is that some works and movements are more interesting than others and that this response can change from individual to individual.

Postmodernism nevertheless deserves credit as a critical theory for its insistence that we cannot just write off the past, that we have to respect the role it played in shaping our cultural institutions and recognise how entrenched it is in our daily lives and experiences in a way that goes beyond mere nostalgia. That also includes the role that modernism has played in that process, since it too is now part of our past, a point that postmodernist theorists perhaps did not take into account as much as they might have (except in the sense of satirical references on 'Picasseau' lines). Altermodernism, however, did, arguing for a broader vision of our aesthetic history that did not see it as a case of one theory or style eradicating another – an attitude that is far too common. Elements of the modern are inevitably around in the postmodern too. Modernism could not be ignored, but it would have to be repositioned in terms of that history (the point Bourriaud was making about postcolonialism). It had changed the cultural landscape in too profound a way to be sidelined as a rather unfortunate mistake, an experiment gone wrong as it were – an opinion one can still hear being made about such as Schoenberg, or James Joyce's *Finnegans Wake* (literature pushed to, or even past, its limits, as its many critics would have it, and not a work designed to draw a mass audience). We had to 'alter' our view of modernism, just as modernists needed to alter theirs of their non-modernist contemporaries. Pluralism was the state to aim for in the arts, with a less judgemental attitude all around.

Jean-François Lyotard's conception of the relationship between the modern and the postmodern also registers a commitment to pluralism in the arts. His argument is – rather counter-intuitively, it has to be said – that the postmodern is a condition that might be said to precede the modern; we might think of it as analogous to the actual process of artistic creation itself, when invention is taking place in a fairly free manner:

> A postmodern artist or writer is in the position of a philosopher: the text he writes, the work he produces are not in principle governed by preestablished rules, and they cannot be judged according to a determining judgment, by applying familiar categories to the text or to the work. Those rules and categories are what the work of art itself is looking for. The artist and the writer, then, are working without rules in order to formulate the rules of what *will have been done*.[7]

It is only once the artwork has been produced that it can be positioned with regard to other works by its critics and audience.

As Lyotard sees it, the creative process is not bound by the dictates of the authorities in the field – or at least should not consider itself to be bound by them. That of course encourages pluralism in terms of artistic expression. It is a view that describes the era of modernism best (and Lyotard's artistic preferences were largely modernist), in the sense of the constant search for originality that motivated its practitioners. But in theory it could describe artistic creation in any era, especially one in which new styles are coming into being that break away from established conventions and critical norms. At such times creative artists are exercising their right to dissent from what is expected from them. It is an idiosyncratic interpretation of the postmodern, but a thought-provoking one that brings it into play as a constant presence in the artistic process, rather than just a reaction to one particular style. It is part of the way we experience the act of creation.

For Lyotard, thought is to be compared to clouds, with ideas forming, re-forming and overlapping as they come to us. There is no fixed identity to them, they contain elements from various sources, including other thinkers, passing freely between individuals: '[T]houghts are not our own. We try to enter into them and to belong to them. What we call the mind is the exertion of thinking thoughts.'[8] It should be mentioned here that intellectual copyright makes no sense from this point of view: whatever you think is to be understood as an amalgam of an ongoing, interactive process with others, all of us reacting to what we have read and what we have heard. Lyotard's conception of the creative process is very similar, meaning that it escapes rules and regulations while it is unfolding, appropriating whatever it needs from whatever source it chooses in order to push the task on. There is a freedom there that cannot be appropriated by the authorities, so that the arts always have the capacity to be used to express dissent. It is not difficult to draw a political message from this, because it does indicate there is a limit to the reach of the authorities, and that can be taken advantage of by dissenters of all persuasions. From this perspective the arts are a naturally pluralist area of activity and that alone makes them suspicious to the authorities, for whom the unpredictability that such diversity brings in its train is a threat to their efforts to maintain control over their society.

Criticism and dissent

Few creative artists welcome criticism, generally regarding it as unhelpful to the practice of their art; good reviews are believed far more than bad ones are (as a writer, I know that temptation only too well). Critics tend to be seen as enemies, with the power to turn the public against the artist's work before they engage with it, and, admittedly, bad reviews can have that effect: one star from a well-regarded critic in a national newspaper will do a film or play no favours. Granted, critics can be petty and ill informed, or prejudiced against a given creative artist's work, but they also play a vital role in terms of the dissent imperative in the arts. Artists are rarely the best judge of their own work, and criticism, painful though it can seem, serves to create new perspectives that can affect how the arts develop, as well as how they are received by the general public. Critical opinions are just that and should not be treated as authoritative, by either the public or the creative artist being written about. Critics can be criticised back and should be (just as critical theorists of different persuasions are by each other), but they are to be considered an essential part of the conversation around the arts in the way that the political opposition is within the parliamentary system. The more debate there is about the arts and the greater the scrutiny of what is being produced for public consumption, then the more that artists are challenged and pushed out of their comfort zone – a form of quality control, as it were, that the arts would be all the poorer without. Artists can become dogmatic too and critical debate is the way to prevent that from happening. As with everything concerning dissent, debate is the crucial component; that is always dissent's primary objective, both in its formal and informal contexts. Disagreement is fine and only to be expected; accusations of false consciousness are not. If you like Schoenberg then go ahead and like Schoenberg, if you like Rachmaninov then feel free to like Rachmaninov. It should not be a contest of wills as to who is right or wrong; that is not the business of aesthetics (although it is a failing of many critics to think that it is).

Adorno was not the first philosopher to suggest that there was a right and a wrong in terms of aesthetic responses, however, as both

David Hume and Immanuel Kant put forward criteria for taste in the arts, in their case to try and establish standards of phenomena such as beauty. Beauty is, for Hume, a matter of sentiment, something 'felt, more properly than perceived', although reason also has a part to play in our response: 'in many orders of beauty, particularly those of the finer arts, it is requisite to employ much reasoning, in order to feel the proper sentiment; and a false relish may frequently be corrected by argument and reflection'.[9] With the appropriate reasoning, all of our fellow human beings could come to the 'correct' appreciation of artistic beauty, which does assume that there is an agreed standard as to what that involves: a clear distinction between a true and a false relish that the initiated can immediately intuit. Adorno would agree with the notion that there is a false relish in musical appreciation: preferring neoclassical Stravinsky to twelve-tone Schoenberg would count as that, for example, although his argument would be directed against the tyranny of taste as someone like Hume understood the concept. The tyranny of taste in Adorno's time preferred the tonality of the past to the atonality of Schoenberg and his disciples (and has largely continued to do so right down to the present day, in popular as well as serious music). To Adorno, this was a bourgeois response, therefore one for Marxists to avoid; the arts were an area of ideological conflict for that constituency. Not all Marxists were to share Adorno's iconoclasm, however, and the authorities were to make it very clear that there was no place for serial composition in the arts life of the newly established Soviet Union, nor for anything else that was in any way stylistically experimental. The two sides had very different ideas as to what constituted false consciousness in this domain.

Kant's philosophy is very much concerned with establishing universal laws, and judgements about works of art follow that principle. Beauty is there to be perceived by everyone, who will (or should) experience the same feeling when confronted by it. As with Hume, there is an assumption of an agreed standard as to what constitutes good art, something universal in its effect. Taste is a shared phenomenon that all can recognise, although as Hume notes, we may well have to work at it to bring ourselves in line with the 'proper sentiment' required, the sentiment approved by the enlightened art-lover. Problems do arise with Kant, however, when it comes to his concept of the sublime, which induces a sense of awe in us because it lies beyond our control and does not conform to our notions of beauty.[10] The sublime, as expressed for example in the force of nature, is capable of frightening and even terrifying us with the power it displays (storms, lightning etc.), although Kant argues that it can also lead to pleasurable experiences. Most commentators are unpersuaded by his attempt to rationalise the sublime, however (poststructuralists and post-modernists particularly), and it has become a powerful symbol of human vulnerability for many thinkers and creative artists, the point where reason can no longer help us.[11] What Kant tried to construct was a complete philosophical scheme in which all our judgements would be based on universal laws, in the arts no less than elsewhere; but the sublime raises questions about the success of such an exercise. In effect, the sublime functions as a dissenting voice within Kant's would-be philosophical grand narrative, as constructed across his three monumental *Critiques*.[12] That is how it is viewed by thinkers like Lyotard, for whom the Kantian sublime irrevocably undermines the claims of rationalist philosophy and thus of the possibility of grand narratives: 'The sublime feeling is neither moral universality nor aesthetic universalization, but is, rather, the destruction of one by the other in the violence of their differend' (a differend being an irreconcilable dispute between incompatible entities).[13] The sublime will resist incorporation into any scheme we might devise. (We might even see the Covid pandemic as a very practical illustration of the sublime in action, destructive intent very much to the fore.)

What is critical with the aesthetic theories of both Hume and Kant is that there are agreed canons for judging artworks, meaning that some works will fail to meet that test and arouse the proper sentiments in their audience. Aesthetics becomes a rule-bound activity and taste a grand narrative that has the last word on artistic merit, which encourages an authoritarian attitude towards artistic creation: if you are rejected by the supposed (most likely self-appointed and socially conservative) arbiters of taste, then you are assumed to have failed in your work. It is the elite's decision that counts. Challenging the status quo becomes very difficult under such circumstances, as modernists could attest by the uproar they generated when they set about breaking the established rules of their respective artforms; but as we have also noted, that has a tendency to promote a new form of authoritarianism in defence of any new style or practice. Adorno's politicised aesthetics is a world away from that of the shared good taste assumed by both Hume and Kant, but all believe their method of judging artworks is the only correct one to adopt, that there is a proper sentiment that must be accessed in such cases. I would argue that this is against the spirit of artistic creation. Freedom of expression is being severely curtailed by such theories, which is the point being made by Lyotard with his conception of the role of the postmodern in aesthetics. It always has to be remembered that taste changes over time and that what constitutes good taste for one generation most likely will not for a later. Bach's reputation has wavered over the centuries, as has Shakespeare's, and may well do so in the future too; aesthetics cannot really offer any universal law on such matters. Even serialism may become popular at some point in the future, preferred by the general public over Stravinsky, Rachmaninov, Sibelius and the like. I would not bet on it myself, but one just never knows how popular taste will develop or what might capture the mood of the times.

The arts and politics

The arts are an important source of political dissent too, and the more the authorities close down opportunities for opposition in the political arena then the more valuable the arts become in that respect. Politicians (particularly authoritarian-minded ones) can very easily become rattled by artworks with a political edge, and obvious examples can be cited of creative artists using their own particular medium to score political points, such as Picasso's *Guernica*, a cry of protest against the actions of the fascist side in the Spanish Civil War and its bombing of innocent civilians in the town of that name in the Basque region. Although critics are divided as to how effective the painting is in protest terms (it is a bit chaotic for some[14]), there is no denying it has been perceived that way by the public and continues to carry a powerful anti-war message wherever it is exhibited. Picasso's contemporary Joan Miró was another to use his art to support the republican side in that war, as in his famous poster *Aidez l'Espagne*, which was circulated widely as a print (deliberately priced cheaply to assist this) and came to symbolise resistance to the fascists. Bertolt Brecht's plays were also highly critical of fascism and right-wing ideology in general, views which forced him into exile when the Nazis came to power in Germany, an event which triggered an exodus of many of the country's creative community (including figures like Adorno).

In totalitarian societies the arts can often become one of the few ways of expressing dissent against the governing regime, although that is always an activity that can turn out to be dangerous, as creative artists in the Soviet Union found out in works like Dmitri Shostakovich's Fourth Symphony (1936), purportedly a portrait of Stalin. With its harsh sonorities and dissonant climaxes the work as a whole sounds like a sustained outburst of anger about how life was developing in Russia in the 1930s, when Stalin was embarked on a programme of eliminating even the suggestion of opposition to his rule (as in the notorious purges of so many of his erstwhile party contemporaries). So savage a portrait was it that it was never performed at the time, nor for the rest of Stalin's life, underlining the difficulties facing those who want to protest against totalitarianism. Shostakovich may have survived Stalinist repression, going in and out of official favour in an unpredictable fashion over the period, but many others in the arts in the Soviet Union were not so fortunate, often dying in prison. That was the fate of the famed theatrical director Vsevolod Meyerhold, for example, accused of not conforming to the dictates of socialist realism, a charge which was used to destroy the careers of many in the Stalinist era. Nevertheless, creative artists have been willing to put themselves on the line in that fashion throughout history and if nothing else their work has kept alive the spirit of dissent within their societies, even if it has been subject to censorship; in fact, censorship merely draws attention to the work in question. The same can definitely be said about John Bunyan, whose most famous work, *The Pilgrim's Progress*, is a landmark of religious dissent that has provided inspiration to generations of readers right up to the present day; its protagonist refuses to give up his beliefs no matter what obstacles the authorities may put in his way, thus turning into a timeless symbol of individual resistance to state power and peer pressure. Interestingly enough, it was never censored by the authorities in England at the time, despite the various restrictions that religious dissenters were having to face under the Restoration regime, so effectively did its allegorical style disguise its subversive political implications.[15] It demonstrated that there are ways around censorship, and that is a powerful message to send out.

Bunyan's narrative can be seen as a response to the culture war being waged by the Restoration regime and that is a position creative artists often find themselves in, as Francis Frascina's book on the role played by prominent artists in 1960s America explores.[16] This was a particularly turbulent period in recent American history, with the Vietnam War dividing opinion nationally and provoking more and more protests from the left, protests which all too frequently generated a violent response from the authorities, who really did regard this a full-scale culture war (as a case in point, the protests at Kent State University in Ohio in 1970 led to several deaths, commemorated in the song 'Ohio' by Neil Young). The creative arts joined in this movement enthusiastically, from art and literature through to the pop music industry, the latter reaching a huge worldwide audience with its message of opposition to the war. There was, as Doug Bradley and Craig Werner's book on the topic describes it, a 'Soundtrack of the Vietnam War'.[17]

It is always difficult to determine how much effect the arts can have on politics, but works that are critical of the ruling ideology, no matter how obliquely this may be expressed, can serve to keep the cause of dissent alive, even in the face of overt official suppression. They become evidence that total control over the population's thought and actions cannot be guaranteed and the works that do this, especially if they manage it cunningly enough to evade censorship, can outlast the ideology that thinks it can outlaw dissent. Important though the arts can be as a means of expressing political dissent, however, it is never a good sign when a society has to rely too heavily on them to provide that service, an indication that ideological repression is being particularly effective – as in the case of the Stalinist Soviet Union. The arts are best seen as an adjunct to politics, not as its replacement; but a necessary adjunct all the same. A society where dissent has to go underground is one that is failing its citizens badly, as well as building up problems that will tax future generations to resolve.

Conclusion: pluralism and aesthetic value

None of the above is meant to suggest that creative artists have to like what other artists do, or to agree with their methods and aims. A universal law of taste is an illusion, one that will fail the test of time if nothing else, even from one generation to the next. Belief in your own work has to play a large part in the creative process and that is at the very least an implicit judgement about its value in relation to the rest of the field. But claiming that what you do, or the style or movement you are working in, is the only valid way of creating is a more contentious matter altogether. There should be a sense of proportion about this and it is fair to say that modernists did not always respect that, being too prone to dub any contemporary production with a hint of the past as reactionary. (An interesting example of that attitude on the contemporary art scene can be found in Tracey Emin's insistence that conceptual art, such as her own, was the way forward for artists now, leading to her criticism that her one-time partner Billy Childish was 'stuck, stuck, stuck', because he still engaged in figurative painting. Childish went on, rather wittily, to proclaim a movement called the 'Stuckists' that upheld the virtues of painting, denying that it was a reactionary artform: 'artists who don't paint aren't artists', as their manifesto provocatively declared.[18]) Adorno's 'false musical consciousness' provides a pertinent demonstration of just how extreme, and hectoring, modernists could be about their aesthetic preferences: one might almost speak of a fundamentalist modernism in such cases, and fundamentalism of any kind is always best avoided. Dissent in aesthetics should be directed against such views, while being careful not to fall into the same trap itself. No style can ever claim to be absolutely definitive, the grand narrative that all should feel compelled to follow in order to be in tune with their times and gain the respect of their peers; perspectives should never be that narrow or restrictive. Authoritarianism ought to have no place in the arts, or in its criticism either; it is an area where pluralism should thrive and that pluralism has important political implications.

The arts can be an object lesson to us, therefore, both in how to identify the growth of authoritarianism and in how to dissent against it. An object lesson, too, in how authoritarianism can emerge even in areas where it would seem to run counter to their ethos. Aesthetics is not a field where authority ought to be playing a leading role, although that is unfortunately what all too often happens, as the discussion above amply illustrates: the tyranny of good taste is a factor that each new generation of creative artists has to deal with. What aesthetics ought to be doing is encouraging difference and diversity rather than being deployed to enforce adherence to a set of rules, or making accusations of false consciousness – surely one of the most dubious and overworked of critical concepts, whether applied to Stravinsky or the Stuckists. It should be realised in the arts, as well as in politics, that we are always 'within opinion' and that any judgement that is made of aesthetic value has to bear witness to that. Opinions should be allowed to flourish, but only if they steer well clear of becoming diktats: socialist realism is fine as long as it is an option, but not when it is an imposition.

Notes

1. Adorno, *Philosophy of Modern Music*, p. 34.
2. Ibid., p. 5.
3. Ibid., p. 7.
4. Ibid., p. 34.
5. See Jencks, *The Language of Post-Modern Architecture*.
6. Bourriaud, 'Altermodern', pp. 12–13.
7. Lyotard, *The Postmodern Condition*, p. 81 (emphasis in original).
8. Lyotard, *Peregrinations*, p. 6.
9. Hume, *Enquiries Concerning Human Understanding and Concerning the Principles of Morals*, pp. 165, 173.
10. See Kant, *Critique of Judgement*.
11. It was used to that effect in the work of Gothic novelists such as Ann Radcliffe (see *The Mysteries of Udolpho* for example).

12. These comprise *Critique of Pure Reason*, *Critique of Practical Reason* and *Critique of Judgement*.
13. Lyotard, *Lessons on the Analytic of the Sublime*, p. 239.
14. 'Nobody knows what is going on in it,' Timothy Hilton has complained (Hilton, *Picasso*, p. 246).
15. For a detailed discussion of these, see Hill, *A Turbulent, Seditious, and Factious People*.
16. Frascina, *Art, Politics and Dissent*.
17. Bradley and Werner, *We Gotta Get Out of This Place*.
18. See 'The Stuckist Manifesto'.

Chapter 7

Internal Dissent: The Case for Self-Critique

It is all too easy for any individual to fall into dogmatism, treating our own beliefs as sacrosanct, whether in politics or elsewhere. Prejudice naturally follows on, especially on the right, but the left can be just as guilty of this trait; communism has left a long and unfortunate legacy to ponder over that will taint left-wing thought and theorising for generations, one suspects. We can see the effect this has on politics, which has of late become ever more polarised in terms of the parties involved in its representative bodies across the democratic system, with a distinctly negative impact on the quality of debate and dialogue both institutionally and publicly; hence the increased resort to cancel culture. Politics declines into a series of theatrical gestures when that happens (the UK parliament is a particularly pertinent, and often very depressing, example of what this can look like in session, particularly at Prime Minister's Question Time), with little meaningful interaction between speakers or parties taking place: producing soundbites seems to be the main concern of the exchanges and the participants invariably oversimplify complex issues in their search for catchy headlines to be picked up by the media. One way to curb the growth of dogmatism would be self-critique, in which we would analyse our own beliefs regularly, and thoroughly, to detect the prejudices they might be hiding – and they are likely to be there in any of us, no matter how socially liberal or 'woke' we might consider ourselves to be. The gap between belief and truth is not always observed as closely as it might be to prevent prejudice from crossing the line in our thought; constant vigilance is required. Examining and judging the validity of our beliefs could do with being turned into a ritual that we perform on a daily or at least weekly basis; we should think of it along the lines of a medical check-up on our opinions, a preventative measure to catch dogmatism at source. The objective would be to bring our inner dissenter into play and I am working on the assumption that most of us are capable of doing that if we put our mind to it (exception has to be made for the conspiracy theory faction, who could only regard this as a crude attempt to silence them).

Earlier examples of the self-critique procedure in religion and communism will be explored below to consider what we can learn from them now. Although it is characteristic in these cases to judge the individual's thought and conduct against a belief system taken to be beyond all possible doubt as to its truth and thus inclined towards dogmatism (as in the case of Maoism, for example, and indeed communism in general), that is not what is being recommended here, as it reduces the scope for meaningful dissent. Dissent must always be directed against those calling for unquestioning belief in their ideological system, because that is never in any society's best interests; it fosters discrimination and a general lack of respect for others' views and lifestyles, and we know how badly that can turn out. Minorities are always at risk in such situations, as the rise of populism makes abundantly clear, given that they are convenient scapegoats for movements actively seeking these to promote their own solidarity – white supremacism, for instance. If we find ourselves drifting that way in an opinion check-up then that is a warning signal that should never be ignored. Do exercise your political agency, but exercise it on behalf of an anti-authoritarian scepticism rather than dogmatism.

Dogma and self-critique: the case of Christianity

Christianity, like any monotheism, has always been resolutely opposed to doubt concerning its beliefs, and its adherents are taught that it is their duty to overcome this in their thinking and to identify where it is they are going wrong by allowing themselves to fall victim to such potentially heretical notions. In Christianity's heyday the assumption was that notions of that kind came from the devil, hence the rise of institutions such as the Inquisition designed to eliminate them, by death if need be: heresy demanded the strongest possible response, otherwise it would infect countless others and constitute a major threat to Christendom. True faith was characterised by an absence of doubt, meaning that even a glimmer of the latter had to be treated as suspect; to voice it was to invite severe recriminations from the authorities, who would most likely interpret it as a case of the devil trying to corrupt you. Even suggesting a different interpretation of doctrine counted as doubt to those in control, as the Cathars, Lollards and Hussites, amongst others, found to their cost. There was little leeway allowed on such matters; obedience was the only acceptable attitude and it took considerable courage to offer a challenge to that.

John Bunyan provides a particularly striking case of Christian internal dissent in his autobiography, *Grace Abounding to the Chief of Sinners*, an unflinching exercise in self-criticism over the issue of the author's prospects for salvation. Styling yourself the 'chief of sinners' hardly suggests much confidence in the outcome, and even if it was already becoming a somewhat cliched phrase by Bunyan's time the evidence is that he truly believed it applied to him. The text records years of intense self-examination of the author's thought and conduct in an attempt to assess the depth of his Christian belief. Bunyan is never completely satisfied that he is showing the signs of salvation and given that he believes in predestination, whereby individuals are marked out by God for salvation or damnation before they are even born (surely religion at its least appealing), this is a matter of the utmost importance to him. His entire future hinges on it and without positive signs he can only expect the worst, as can the majority of humankind in the more extreme interpretations of the theory, where God hands out salvation very sparingly. The suffering this causes him, both mentally and physically, is acute, often rendering him all but unable to cope with normal daily life:

> Then was I struck into a very great trembling, insomuch that at some times I could for whole days together feel my very body as

well as my mind to shake and totter under the sense of the dreadful judgement of God . . . I felt also such a clogging and heat at my stomach by reason of this my terror, that I was, especially at some times, as if my breast-bone would have split in sunder.[1]

The only point of reference that Bunyan allows himself is the Bible, and his narrative is a series of tests that he conducts on himself to decide whether or not his faith is true, in which he constantly pores over and parses key passages of the Bible at length to see what they can tell him about his condition. In his mind what these tests usually reveal is that he is falling short of what is required, sometimes drastically short, and this consistently destabilises his character. Bunyan even speaks of his 'tempter' frequently mocking him over this repeated realisation of the utter hopelessness of his spiritual condition: '[H]e strongly suggested to me, that I ought not to pray to God, for prayer was not for any in my case, neither could it do me good.'[2] He is, after all, the 'chief of sinners' and cannot expect God ever to regard him as a suitable candidate for Heaven. As self-critique goes it is gruelling, picturing someone who in modern terms of reference is regularly collapsing into episodes of deep depression and whose personality overall is probably describable as being bipolar. The depressive states are often broken by feelings of elation at reading an apparently comforting passage from the Bible, but these rarely last for very long: 'down fell I, as a bird that is shot from the top of a tree, into great guilt and fearful despair' is an entirely typical experience.[3] A sense of desperation at his plight haunts the narrative and its tortuous journey towards a state of assumed 'grace'.

There are times in reading this kind of material when being a religious dissenter can seem like being at the centre of an elaborate conspiracy run by God. There are no accidents on view in this world either, nothing happens by chance and all you can do as a lone, vulnerable individual is try to make whatever sense you can of the plan lying behind it, frantically analysing all the signs you are receiving in the hope that they will start to turn your way, forlorn though that outcome might usually appear to be. Someone else is clearly calling the shots: an extremely dispiriting situation to find oneself caught up in, especially with the dreadful possibility of eternal damnation as one of the options God might have chosen for you. And not just one option, but the likeliest, as theologians of the time who believed in predestination tended to argue. Those selected would, according to one such (Arthur Dent, whose work influenced Bunyan), 'walke very thinly in the streets': not a message calculated to inspire a great deal of hope in the average reader, one suspects.[4] Spiritual success seems the most remote of possibilities.

There is an ideal of behaviour that Bunyan is measuring himself against that he cannot seem to reach, meaning that there is a dogmatic aspect to this exercise in self-critique. He is in a state of severe doubt as to his character, but that doubt does not extend to the Bible or the belief system that it outlines so confidently: these are constants that Bunyan cannot allow himself to be truly sceptical about. Any such thoughts that may arise, even if only briefly, are merely evidence to him of his unfitness for grace: a case of his malicious tempter at work again. His mental turmoil signals failings in his character, not in Christianity and the demands it is making on him; such demands are only what every believer must expect, given that they are all guilty of original sin against God and therefore deserve no mercy at all to be shown towards them. Scepticism calls for a much more open-minded form of internal dissent than Bunyan engages in, for all the massive psychological effort that he devotes to it. As with communism, there are limits as to how far the internal dissent is permitted to go; your belief system is an implacable barrier that allows no room for manoeuvre. Eventually that effort pays off, however, and Bunyan comes to feel that the Bible is telling him he is going to be one of the saved: 'Now did my chains fall off my legs indeed, I was loosed from my afflictions and irons, my temptations also fled away.'[5] In his sense it is therefore a successful piece of self-criticism and self-critique, if a distinctly harrowing one to have gone through. Being a Christian comes across as more than something of an ordeal, a relentless test of one's character that pushes it to its limits.

The Pilgrim's Progress provides us with a fictionalised version of that anxiety-laden experience, with the protagonist Christian engaged in a protracted struggle against both his own psychology and his society's ruling ideology and customs, until he finds himself accepted into the ranks of the saved in Heaven. It is a triumph for dissent and therefore for the theology that inspired it. Christian refuses to follow the social norms and live the quiet, orderly life expected of him as one of the masses. Ignorance, the more conventionally religious figure who is an occasional companion of Christian on the journey, one smugly confident of his salvation as a law-abiding, regular churchgoer (Anglican, one has to assume), is rudely dispatched to Hell from Heaven's gates just to reinforce the dissenting message. In its own terms of reference dissent is being recognised in the only way it considers to be of any real significance; salvation makes all your suffering worthwhile. Christian's wife, Christiana, and their children, left behind by him in the City of Destruction in the narrative's opening stages, undergo their own successful pilgrimage in Part Two of the work. They show how dissent could grow as a social movement, how it could become a community maintained by its faith and refusal to conform to Anglican worship, as it was to go on and do in the post-Restoration period when religious toleration was instituted.[6] Dissent was to become normalised within English society (even Christiana is assured that the country's citizenry is 'much more moderate now' than in her husband's time[7]), paving the way for more dissent from within its own ranks and the establishment of new sectarian movements.

Even Christians who are willing to entertain doubt about the beliefs themselves, such as René Descartes, who hypothesised himself as the subject of an elaborate game played on him by 'an evil spirit, who is supremely powerful and intelligent, and does his utmost to deceive me', eventually feel compelled to reach a conclusion that proves the validity of their faith: '[T]he conclusion must be: from the mere fact that I exist, and have in me some idea of a most perfect being, that is, God, it is clearly demonstrated that God also exists.'[8] Descartes considers the 'must' to be a product of his philosophical reasoning, but it is his Christian belief that is really pushing him towards his conclusion; his scepticism has to be curtailed by that, otherwise he too would be lapsing into heresy. No 'evil spirit', no matter how malevolent, could triumph over God for very long; it would sound uncomfortably close to the Manichean worldview to entertain such a thought, and Catholicism's uncompromising position on that had been made very plain for centuries beforehand. As with Bunyan, Descartes's self-critique has limits that no true believer, whether a philosopher or not, will feel they can go beyond. It always has to be remembered that it is the believer who is being tested, not the belief system; only the former is fallible.

From Protestant times onwards, Christianity encouraged self-critique on the part of its believers more and more, with spiritual autobiography in the style of Bunyan becoming a regular feature of the dissenting lifestyle, a means of expressing one's inner anxieties so that others could understand the effort required in trying to conform to God's will.[9] The process can also be seen at work in the popularity of the meditational genre in the seventeenth and eighteenth centuries, and particularly the 'resolve' literature within that genre. Resolve literature was about examining one's thought and conduct with a view to becoming a better example of a Christian, one who would constantly be trying to overcome their failings in order to be living as God would want them to. Such works continued to be published into the nineteenth century ('devotional steady sellers', as they have come to be known) and were clearly perceived to be extremely useful aids to determine the depth of one's Christian beliefs, as well as one's fitness for election – an issue, as we have seen, of overriding importance to believers in the genre's heyday in England. One commentator argues that 'devotional steady sellers must be reckoned a – perhaps *the* – canon of popular reading in the early modern West'.[10] The point of these steady sellers was to inspire an internal dialogue in their readers, offering them a standard against which to measure their conduct and a sense that with enough application they too could improve themselves; as the eminent seventeenth-century preacher and theologian Richard Baxter neatly put it, to meditate was to induce a state of 'pleading . . . with thyself' and that was to be seen as an ongoing project.[11]

The resolve genre was not as angst-ridden as the work of spiritual autobiographers such as Bunyan, suggesting that grace was a far more attainable state than his self-critique was telling him – if the individual was willing to work at it, that is. Resolve manuals sound far closer to modern therapy techniques in their approach, genuinely wanting to help the individual lead a better, more useful life and overcome his or her bad habits, thus becoming a role model for others. Their practical nature is one of their main selling points. It would not be so difficult to set up a resolve system with prejudice and bigotry as the bad habits to be overcome, relying on the same kind of internal dialogue to work through the issues involved. What is needed for such an exercise is the conviction of Bunyan's self-analysis, minus the faith-driven ideal of behaviour that lies behind it. Resolve could easily take on such a sectarian character.

Dogma and self-critique: the case of communism

Communists are just as critical of doubt as religious monotheists, once again putting the blame on the individual for any such lapse of belief: faith in the theory is meant to prevail in both instances, without exception. Degrees of belief are not acceptable; you are either a true believer or you are not – and if you are not then you are sliding towards heresy. It is the party member's duty to bring their views into line with the official creed; not to do so is to turn into an enemy of the movement, which depends on solidarity of belief and unwavering commitment to the party's programme. Self-criticism was devised as a method of ensuring such commitment, being extensively used in the Soviet Union under the rule of Stalin and then later adopted by Mao in China.[12]

Communists were particularly concerned to prevent capitalist or liberal ideas creeping into members' thought and behaviour, hence the accusations so freely thrown around in the days of Mao's Cultural Revolution in the 1960s that certain party members – often high up in the hierarchy – were in fact 'running dogs of capitalism' rather than communist true believers. (It is particularly ironic that the Chinese Communist Party has since developed its own brand of capitalist enterprise in the country and trades freely with its one-time bitter enemy, the Western capitalist order, to the extent that its economy is critically dependent upon this arrangement.) The implication was that unless party members policed their thought very carefully, then they were vulnerable to such lapses and that they were guilty of a serious lack of discipline for allowing it to happen. Mao described what was needed in typically practical terms:

> Conscientious practice of self-criticism is still another hallmark distinguishing our Party from all other political parties. As we say, dust will accumulate if a room is not cleaned regularly, our faces will get dirty if they are not washed regularly. Our comrades' minds and our Party's work may also collect dust, and also need sweeping and washing.[13]

The purity of communist belief had to be maintained and it was to be considered as always under threat at the individual level; that was the movement's weak point. Everything a member did ought to be examined closely by that individual to check that he or she had not been infected by anti-communist ideas, which were of course dominant outside the communist bloc and keen to undermine its system. If a member could be shown to have been so infected (capitalism playing the tempting devil role in this case) then a public confession of guilt was required, with the Cultural Revolution leading to a rash of these as the party turned inward on itself in a purge of the supposedly ideologically unreliable. Communist regimes can become more than somewhat paranoid about this threat within their ranks, so self-critique was expected to be a standard part of the communist lifestyle, without which it would be at risk of being infiltrated by capitalist ideology in what was a culture war on an international scale. Once again the belief system is taken to be sacrosanct and you are expected to conform to its standards in terms of your behaviour. As with religion, there is no room for negotiation on such issues, nor any sense that being 'within opinion' is an option; the only acceptable outcome is to conform to the party line. Whether or not this is a travesty of Marx's thought, as many of his supporters have claimed down the years, is open to debate, but not within the communist movement. Communist states do not have official opposition parties in their ruling bodies.

Psychoanalysis and the ideology of self-critique

Psychoanalysis is designed to encourage self-critique, expecting analysands to ponder over the sessions with the psychoanalyst afterwards on their own, rather than just telling them how to change their behaviour to overcome whatever it is that is troubling them. The analysand is supposed to be an active participant in his or her treatment, which will not be very effective otherwise, or at least not lastingly so. Internal change is what is required, a resetting of one's outlook with the aim of functioning better in the world, and that has to be an exercise in honest and thorough self-analysis in the manner of resolve literature.

The model of well-adjustedness that lies behind the psychoanalytical process has, however, been criticised by various theorists, perhaps most notably, and notoriously, by Gilles Deleuze and Félix Guattari in their books *Anti-Oedipus* and *A Thousand Plateaus*. For these theorists there is an underlying ideology to the form of self-critique that psychoanalysis is promoting – effectively that of advanced capitalism. What the system wants from every individual is conformity, with no questions being asked of how it operates, and psychoanalysis is part of the repressive mechanism by which this conformity is imposed on all of us: 'Oedipus' as the authors style it. Self-critique under this regimen becomes a means of policing ourselves to ensure that we do not deviate from the norms of our society; in other words, to prevent dissent from ever being formulated and the system's validity being called into question. The resolve here is to be the same as everyone else so that we pose no threat at all to those in control, whose preferred mode of behaviour for the rest of us, as in Bunyan's world, is obedience. Deleuze and Guattari put forward schizophrenia as an antidote to this conditioning, daring us to act in such an unpredictable manner that the system is dumbfounded by it and has no clear idea how best to respond – certainly not to any mass outbreak of the phenomenon. What they are recommending would amount to a full-scale campaign of civil disobedience against the Western capitalist order and the assumptions on which it is based, such as that it is our duty to be productive and that we should never question our culture's parameters, particularly its socio-economic ones (neoliberalism continues this tradition into our own day). Productive work is to be regarded as our destiny, with our social and political masters reaping the benefit: precisely the situation that Marx was so incensed about in his work.

R. D. Laing and the 'anti-psychiatry' movement were similarly motivated to challenge the goals of their discipline (although Laing himself did not like the 'anti-psychiatry' tag), identifying an ideal type of personality behind those goals that did not represent the full range of human experience. Schizophrenia, for example, was to be considered a valid form of experience rather than an illness or a madness; it should not be thought of as something to be cured. Laing is, to say the least, provocative in his view of the repressive effect of our society, speaking of the 'present pervasive madness that we call normality, sanity, freedom' and of how 'psychiatry can so easily be a technique of brainwashing, of inducing behaviour that is adjusted'.[14] Such ideas are at the very least highly controversial and might be said to push dissent to the extreme; but they nevertheless succeed in raising questions about the impact of ideology on the relevant disciplines and how this can encourage the development of dogmatic attitudes. Is it perhaps the system that requires adjusting, not the individual? That is a question dissent will find itself asking over and over again when facing up to the demands of authority.

Pressure to conform to conventional codes of behaviour is something that all of us are subject to at various points in our life and in most cases we do conform, even if it proves to be a stressful exercise. The system depends upon that response, the product of our social conditioning from childhood onwards, from family, friends, schooling and the workplace: as Laing puts it, we construct 'a false self to adapt to false realities', almost as if schizophrenia is built into the social contract.[15] When any social trend threatens those conventions in a really meaningful way, as in the case of the hippie movement in the 1960s and its call to 'tune in, turn on and drop out', then it is noticeable how worried the authorities become and how quickly they take action to curb it. The implications of any such refusal to stick to the social and political rules is not lost on the authorities, who recognise it as an existential threat to the system they control: a system that depends on self-policed and self-maintained conformity.

Jacques Derrida also puts forward some typically provocative ideas on the rationale for psychoanalysis and the assumptions it makes, identifying what he calls the 'resistances of psychoanalysis' itself to providing authoritative solutions, which is the kind of opening that dissent is always on the lookout for.[16] As usual in Derrida's work, the point is to demonstrate that no theory can ever be in total control of its material, that it will never deliver certainty because of the unavoidable amount of 'play' in it. Projections will always fall foul of this phenomenon. Rather as John Barrow does on science, Derrida is insisting that there are limits to what psycho-analysis can do, mysteries that it can never resolve.

Derrida also makes the cogent point that any of us is capable of engaging in the act of self-analysis:

> The fact that I have never been in analysis, in the institutional sense of the analytic situation, does not mean that I am not, here or there . . . analysand and analyst in my own time and in my own way. Like everyone else.[17]

I would query the 'everyone else', however, because if we are all capable of this, not all of us choose to practise it – as in the case of conspiracy theorists.

Feminism, patriarchy and self-critique

Patriarchy is yet another area where there is a wilful refusal to subject beliefs to internal scrutiny, with feminism providing the dissenting voice against the unjustified assumption of authority this invariably involves. Feminist theory calls on both women and men to examine their beliefs and behaviour very closely to determine the extent to which they could be said to be complicit in patriarchy. Self-critique should lead directly to dissent against social norms in this case, since feminism is calling into question an entire way of life that privileges one part of the population at the expense of the other in a manner that falls far short of the ideals of democracy. Much of what this involves went largely unquestioned before modern feminism came on the scene, so well entrenched was it within the social fabric by centuries of tradition (which it still is in many parts of the non-Western world). Feminist theory rejected the practices this had given rise to, arguing the case for equal pay and equal opportunities, as well as an end to outmoded male attitudes of social and sexual domination. In the forthright words of the French feminist theorist Luce Irigaray, '[s]exual difference is one of the major philosophical issues, if not the issue, of our age', one that all women are well aware of in their daily dealings, where the glass ceiling is still a very significant factor in many areas and the threat of male violence always there in the background.[18] Empty promises of reforms and changes to culture are all too prevalent on this topic (almost every government is guilty of this to at least some degree), as they are with race as well.

Opposition to feminism is still common in liberal democracies, however, with arguments regularly trotted out about it being unfair to use positive discrimination in either employment or the political world (equal representation for male and female candidates on party election lists, for example). Once again, however, I do not think that can qualify as dissent, given that it comes from those who benefit from patriarchy, and, as with racism, misogyny is an appeal to prejudice, thus authoritarian in its implications. Another case of fake dissent, I would argue, as it surely is in cases like Turning Point and their categorisation of gender equality as a left-wing plot (one that I was presumably a member of in my time as a university lecturer, thankfully before Turning Point came on the scene). Patriarchy ought to be no more acceptable in a democracy than white supremacism, but the far right are highly resistant to action being taken against such beliefs, falling back on the free speech argument as a means of deflecting any criticism. Free speech in this case means the right to call your opponents 'feminazis'. It is understandable why cancel culture becomes so tempting in such instances, but it is an option that should be resisted nevertheless, because it enables the far right to play the victim card. Wearing though it is, debate about what the limits of free speech should be have to go on being conducted with this constituency (as it must over their equally mean-spirited treatment of the LGBT movement).

Harking back to the issue of aesthetic dissent, it is worth noting that it was a dissenting act for women to become authors until very recently. Literature was deemed to be a male preserve, hence the decision of Charlotte Brontë to adopt the (male-sounding) pseudonym Currer Bell, when publishing her novels.[19] She was only one of several to feel the need to do that in order to be taken seriously by the reading public and to deflect biased criticism (her sisters Anne and Emily chose Acton Bell and Ellis Bell respectively, with Mary Anne Evans opting for George Eliot), even though there had been many well-known and widely read women novelists before her in the eighteenth and early nineteenth century, Frances Burney, Jane Austen and Ann Radcliffe being particularly notable examples. Patriarchy still regarded it as against the natural order of things for women to challenge male authority in this area and it was family pressure as much as anything that had to be resisted; wives and daughters were just not supposed to put themselves forward in that way, it was considered unseemly. Although Burney's father, the noted musicologist Dr Charles Burney, supported her desire to publish her first novel, *Evelina*, he was to insist that she did so anonymously in order to observe social decorum (nor was she the only female novelist of the time to adopt that practice). Women have had the same sort of problem breaking into other traditionally male preserves, such as film-directing, which is slowly coming to adjust to the idea. But it needs strong character in every case to dissent from conventional behaviour; as always, elites do not give up their privileges at all easily.

Race and self-critique

Black Lives Matter (BLM) has loudly broadcast a message of the urgent need for self-critique on issues of race to an international audience. This became particularly evident during the 2020 US presidential election, when the movement maintained a high profile that gained extensive news coverage. White supremacism was effectively mainstreamed and normalised during the Trump presidency, and that this could happen makes it one of the most crucial areas for dissent to address. The furore over the death of George Floyd brought this normalisation to the forefront of public consciousness through the actions of American police departments, which received enthusiastic support from President Trump and his followers for their blatantly violent tactics. Several deaths of black people at the hands of the police have followed on from the Floyd case, underlining that it was no mere anomaly, or just a case of a rogue officer or two (as critics had tended to dismiss such incidents in the past). Dissent against this has to mean street protests, where the hostility of the authorities registers very clearly as they invariably do their best to turn it into an issue of law and order, thus refusing to acknowledge the moral imperative behind the actions: authoritarianism just does not recognise protest. It is yet another inexcusable incidence of denialism, allowing no space for debate, thus a defence of the normalisation of discrimination. If enough of a public outcry results, then such authorities will, usually grudgingly, promise to do something about it; but such promises are all too rarely kept. BLM, however, has made it much more difficult to avoid such issues indefinitely and that is to be welcomed. It is a good example of what Roland Bleiker described as the transnational quality that dissent has taken on in modern times, where '[t]he presence of mass media can transform a local act of resistance almost immediately into an event of global significance'.[20] This can be seen in the impact the movement has made in the sports world, with so many players across a wide range of spectator sports around the world 'taking the knee' before games (politically divisive though this has proved to be, particularly, as one would expect, in the US). As a result, the general public are constantly being reminded of the issue and most likely will be for quite some time to come yet.

BLM's campaign against police brutality raises far wider questions about the state of liberal democracy in countries such as the US and that is exactly what dissent should be doing. Their call to defund the police envisages a very different kind of social set-up than the one now in place, where the American prison population is disproportionately made up of black men. Police brutality is merely the most obvious sign of far deeper problems in American life, of the institutional failings that allow racism to thrive. The public debate about how to address these failings is long overdue and it really has to get down to the individual level.

Self-psychiatry and self-psychoanalysis

If all of us were to engage in really rigorous self-critique of our beliefs on a regular basis, in effect to be our own psychiatrist and psychoanalyst, pleading with ourselves to avoid prejudice and bigotry in all our dealings with others, then authoritarianism would find it far harder to take root in our culture. The same would go for conspiracy theories, which are highly unlikely to survive any prolonged system of testing if it is approached with the requisite seriousness and intellectual rigour; that is to say, without any policy-based evidence-making being allowed in to distort the process. The growth of authoritarianism is the fault not primarily of the politicians who close down dissent, spread prejudice and amass as much power as possible to themselves, but of those who believe the narrative they spin and then uncritically do what it tells them to. Politicians like Donald Trump are prone to making wild statements about what they have achieved, as well as condemning all criticism of their record as being based on fake news, claims that almost never add up; yet if it were not the case that a significant proportion of the public unquestioningly takes this at face value, then it would not do the damage that it patently is doing (that seventy-four million Americans did this in the 2020 presidential election is a very sobering thought; that a majority of them actually do believe the election was stolen from them by a Democrat-organised conspiracy is even more sobering). There will probably always be autocratically inclined politicians coming forward, they have after all a long and unpleasant history behind them to draw on for role models; but we do not have to believe them and thus pave their way to power – and more importantly, abuse of that power. The answer to authoritarianism lies in us, not in trying to prevent mavericks from vying for our attention by playing on our prejudices; that is yet another phenomenon which has a presence in all ages. As Pragya Agarwal has pointed out, those prejudices may be the product of 'unconscious' bias, but that still 'cannot excuse discriminatory behaviour', which can be brought to the surface by a process of 'unravelling' the 'sway' we might be experiencing towards particular biases, which can then be corrected.[21] The way to counter the sway towards the far right is to address it at the individual level and that is a task all of us ought to be prepared to undertake; in terms of contemporary cultural developments it should be considered a priority. As Agarwal notes, it can be said of all of us that '[w]e often ignore details that contradict our existing beliefs', but it would appear to be an article of faith on the far right to do so each and every time it happens.[22] (I would emphasise that this is not an attack on right-wing politics or attitudes, even though I do not myself agree with them, but their far-right version only. There are correspondences between them, but I concede that in the main the right are supporters of liberal democracy and adhere to its principles – even if rather patronisingly on occasion. It soon becomes apparent when a shift to extremism takes place, as Trumpism seems to be effecting in the Republican Party in one of the more unwelcome developments in recent political history in the West. Some serious self-critique is long overdue within the party.)

The first question to ask ourselves in self-critique ought to be, am I being gullible? By contrast, when it comes to both Christian and communist self-critique the first question would seem to be, am I being unfaithful to the creed? That is something to keep a very watchful eye out for, since only you as an individual can alter your behaviour to prevent it from happening: that would be facing up to the lure of the sway with positive intent. The next stage of course would be to resolve not to let that happen again in the future, to construct an internal system of vigilance for identifying it and defusing it at source. Any of us is capable of being taken in on occasion so we must go on asking ourselves that question and scrutinising the basis of our beliefs, cultivating an inner dialogue about their validity or otherwise. Politicians spouting prejudice can only get away with it if we accept what they say as truth and do not investigate what lies behind their claims (and 'lies' is very much the operative word here). We must always be on the lookout for gullibility, or perhaps it would be less provocative to call it susceptibility; we must be prepared to ask ourselves awkward questions about our personal ideological biases and whether they represent 'false realities'. We have to be exceedingly careful that we are asking ourselves the right questions; crucially, ones free of policy-based evidence-making. It is a case of being permanently sceptical, in other words, always aware that our learned responses from the past may cause us to slip up, creating what I have referred to elsewhere as an 'internal differend' (often with our very own 'inner conspiracy theorist', complete with the 'deep-rooted angers' such figures build up, as the antagonist).[23] Being sceptical is the proper starting point from which to campaign against the authoritarian impulse and thereby keep dissent alive, and performing its vital task, in our culture; as Lasana Harris has argued, prejudiced behaviour can be 'unlearned', both in ourselves and in others.[24] Identity politics provides a critical example of just how important it is to 'unlearn' our prejudices, since they are a response to oppression which often has at least the tacit support of large sections of the public. The LGBT movement keeps reminding us of this uncomfortable fact, as do a whole series of ethnic minorities being discriminated against across the globe. Black Lives Matter could qualify as identity politics, although just to complicate matters, so might white supremacism. Once again, however, it is important to determine what drives the politics; anything that is based on bigotry, as white supremacism clearly is, is to be opposed.

A thriving democracy depends on authority at all levels, from the government on down, being kept under pressure and having to explain in detail the rationale for its actions. The less authority likes it, the more necessary it is, because that rationale can all too often turn out to be remarkably shaky and more to do with self-aggrandisement than the public good – and there is never a shortage of authority figures who are guilty of that failing. Dismissing all criticism of their actions and policies as fake news only reveals the weakness of those in power. It is an admission that they have no basis for debate on the issue in question, that all they can do is to shout it down and intimidate their political opponents. Dissent has to keep calling attention to the drift to the far right that such behaviour so ominously signals. It is disturbing to note how ready the far right's supporters are to take fake news at face value – such as the supposedly 'stolen' 2020 election. Elections have indeed been stolen in many one-party states around the world in recent history, with no lack of evidence to back up the accusation, and the US has generally been in the forefront to complain about this undemocratic practice. But the claim about it being perpetrated in America in 2020 is evidence-free – unless one believes that every judge who dismissed the Trump camp's barrage of lawsuits in a series of state courts in the election's immediate aftermath was also a party to the conspiracy. QAnon supporters would have no difficulty believing that the American judicial system was rigged against them in that fashion, however, and the 'steal' seems set to go into popular mythology and have an effect on future elections (2024 looms worryingly in that respect, no matter who the Republican candidate may be). Conspiracy theory is fine when it is used as a basis for fictional narratives (there was a certain vogue for it amongst postmodernist novelists in the 1980s and 1990s, for example[25]), but not when it becomes a method of political analysis in the real world: we really are being presented with false realities when that happens.

Bringing to light our own unconscious biases and examining them can, admittedly, be an uncomfortable exercise, because they are often an integral part of our character, as when one identifies a bias against particular nationalities that is common to one's compatriots. Scots tend to have a bias against the English, for example, based on a long history of animosity, and frequently open warfare, between the two nations, as well as the nature of the power relations within the Union since it was instituted in the eighteenth century. Growing up in Scotland one becomes used to hearing disparaging remarks against the English and in time these can turn into a reflex response of one's own. England has always been by far the leading player in the Union, its greater population and wealth all but guaranteeing this, and that has rankled down the years with many Scots, who can often feel taken for granted in political terms (Brexit was taken as proof of this by many after its conclusive rejection by the electorate there). The resurgence of support for Scottish independence in recent years draws on the feelings engendered by being a small nation under the control of a much larger one, and it can express itself as bias; a reaction to the inferiority complex that such situations can give rise to, perhaps? While understandable on a political level, it can hardly be condoned on a personal one, but it generates jokes and critical asides which serve to reinforce the bias (being a Scot in England will let you see the other side of this, jokes and critical asides about the Scottish character).

Scotland versus England is only one of many such examples that could be cited from around the world, none of which improves the quality of public discourse; rather they tend to keep resentments – real and imagined – simmering away under the surface as an unexamined internal differend, just waiting for an excuse to assert itself and so continue the cycle of bias and prejudice that is so characteristic of nationalism in general. And an excess of nationalism almost invariably ushers in populist politics with all its unsavoury beliefs and practices; there is a natural affinity between them, with evidence being made to fit belief and appeals to prejudice the common parlance. At that point we really do need an opinion check-up to take place and as widely as possible; each of us, as Derrida observed, has in our 'own way' to take account of our personal unconscious biases.

Conclusion: avoiding dogma and authoritarianism

There is a history of self-critique, therefore, and even if it is conducted under the aegis of dogma and authoritarianism, as I am arguing is the case with both the Christian and communist versions, sincerely undertaken though they may be, then we can still learn from that about what it is prudent to avoid in the exercise. Scepticism does not work when it is on behalf of dogma and authoritarianism, only when it is a genuinely open-minded, and open-ended, scrutiny of the basis of beliefs, a thorough investigation into what forms our opinions and whether we can justify holding them. When faith comes on the scene that cannot happen, because the beliefs dictate what the result has to be and shape how the critique develops; as it does with conspiracy theory no less than religion, as the QAnon phenomenon amply proves.

There just has to be a paedophile ring operating behind the scenes, you are not supposed to question this 'fact'. Taking things on trust in that way is alien to the sceptical ethos, which will always want to draw attention to the adverse effect that uncritical belief is having on society. While it is possible to be both religious and critical, it is by no means the norm. Being on the far right and critical, however, would appear to be a contradiction in terms; being on the far right and a conspiracy theorist as well compounds that problem to a socially dangerous degree. A society run by a QAnon political party does not bear thinking about.

Notes

1. Bunyan, *Grace Abounding to the Chief of Sinners*, p. 42.
2. Ibid., p. 45.
3. Ibid., p. 37.
4. Dent, *The Plaine Mans Path-Way to Heaven*, p. 287.
5. Bunyan, *Grace Abounding to the Chief of Sinners*, p. 59.
6. John Seed, in *Dissenting Histories: Religious Division and the Politics of Memory in Eighteenth-Century England*, posits a 'narrative identity' that he argues helped to give a sense of communal history to such a diverse group of sects, from the advent of toleration through the next century.
7. Bunyan, *The Pilgrim's Progress*, p. 256.
8. Descartes, *Philosophical Writings*, pp. 65, 90.
9. For some other examples of the genre, see Bunyan, *Grace Abounding: With Other Spiritual Autobiographies*.
10. Brown, 'The Thick Style', p. 69.
11. Baxter, *The Saints' Everlasting Rest*, p. 271.
12. For the development of self-criticism in the Soviet system see Priestland, *The Red Flag*.
13. Mao, *Quotations from Chairman Mao Tse-tung*, p. 259.
14. Laing, *The Divided Self*, pp. 11, 12.
15. Ibid., p. 12.
16. Derrida, *Resistances of Psychoanalysis*.
17. Ibid., p. 68.
18. Irigaray, *An Ethics of Sexual Difference*, p. 5.
19. See Brontë, *Jane Eyre*, for example, which includes a facsimile of the original title page crediting Currer Bell as being the editor of a supposedly autobiographical text.
20. Bleiker, *Popular Dissent, Human Agency and Global Politics*, p. 1.
21. Agarwal, 'Exposing unconscious bias', p. 42.
22. Agarwal, *Sway*.
23. See Sim, *Lyotard and Politics*, pp. 79–81.
24. See Harris and Cossins, 'The roots of racism'.

25. 'A second meaning of "plot" is that of a secret plan or conspiracy to accomplish a criminal or illegal purpose. The protagonist of the postmodernist novel sometimes suspects that he or she is trapped at the centre of an intrigue, often with some justification' (Lewis, 'Postmodernism and Fiction', p. 177).

Conclusion:
The Dissent Project

The point of my argument overall is that dissent ought to be enthusiastically encouraged in all areas of our culture, given that it keeps authority under constant scrutiny and resists any tendency it might display towards authoritarianism and totalitarianism. The latter is an all too common occurrence with large organisations possessing controlling rights over their area of interest, in the public and private sector alike, and claiming an almost divine right to do as they please there. Several examples of this trait have been considered throughout this book, each with its own characteristics and objectives yet a common sense of purpose, to entrench itself by marginalising any opposition or competition; but a host of others will come to mind for almost anyone willing to ponder the issue even for just a few moments. Centralised power gravitates towards absolute power all too easily and there have to be robust checks and balances in operation to prevent that process from being allowed to run its course, bringing prejudice and bigotry in its wake and a general coarsening of our social existence. There has been more than enough of the latter of late courtesy of the Trump presidency and Brexit. Dissent could be conceived, therefore, as a project designed to preserve liberal democratic ideals through its cultivation of an oppositional imperative; it is what stands between us and autocracy and fascism, and the various ways to keep it alive and functioning that the study has identified, plus the social and political implications they involve, will be summed up in this concluding chapter.

The rationale for dissent

Without dissent, authority will be given free rein to impose itself on its citizens, and it is never in a democracy's interest for that situation to be allowed to develop, let alone become the norm: unmistakable harm will almost inevitably be the consequence for many in the community in that event, with minority groups and immigrants being first in line to suffer. If a crisis is severe enough to warrant the imposition of emergency powers and, crucially, to be perceived that way by the general public, not just the ruling authorities with a vested interest in this move, then such powers should only last as long as the crisis does and protocols should be in place to guarantee that is what happens. This is an obvious point to make perhaps, but one that nevertheless can turn out to be a source of tense political struggle as regimes dig in to preserve their power and privilege without the hindrance of scrutiny, using appeals to prejudice to build up a core support against critics. The pandemic has been an object lesson in that regard. Democracies can easily 'die' unless they can maintain a healthy climate of dissent to curb the ever-present threat of authoritarian tendencies and this cannot be sidelined indefinitely. Trumpism alone should tell us why, as it is beginning to sound more like a cult than a political party, a natural home for extremists of the QAnon kind, who are capable of doing immense damage to the system with their wildly improbable conspiracy theories and outright lies. When dissent is outlawed, even criminalised (as in the examples outlined in Chapters 1 and 2), then warning bells have to begin to sound, and fast; it means that authoritarianism is on the march. Opposition cannot be treated as an optional extra to the democratic political process; it is its lifeblood. Dissent's legitimacy should never be in question; nor should recognition ever be withheld from it by the authorities. For the sake of liberal democracy, dissent always has to be seen and heard, to be capable of accessing the public space it needs to make its points. As Judith Butler has summed it up, 'the very granting of the right of dissent, although an act of power, is also an act in which power checks itself'.[1] When that happens, it constitutes a crucial affirmation of democratic principles.

Contributions to the dissent project can come from any walk of life and this study has been an invitation to become as actively involved in it as possible, permanently on the lookout for abuse of power and the devious ways this can disguise itself. Permanently aware too of the possibility of unconscious bias creeping into our judgements (triggered by our very own 'inner conspiracy theorist' perhaps), as well as the lure that uncritical belief can cast of not being an outsider. Dissent is to be thought of as an attitude of mind as much as anything else, a generalised sense of wariness and scepticism towards the workings of authority and the willingness to give voice to this and refuse to back down, even when such a display of intellectual disobedience might well turn one into an outsider. Dissent always carries that danger, but it has to be embraced nevertheless; better to be an outsider than a member of a community of conspiracy theorists. It pays not to put too much faith in human nature and its disposition towards contributing to the public good; the insidious appeal of power can always distort this, hence the need to keep challenging its practices and forcing it to examine and explain these, whether in the realm of the arts and sciences or that of politics and religion. Becoming a leader in any field can very easily encourage a turn towards authoritarianism and a belief that only one's views are right; that is a tendency which should never go unopposed, particularly in politics, otherwise dictatorships are prone to develop. Dissenters have a duty to keep speaking to future ages about the potential that always exists for this to occur – the more warning voices there are the better. Do not let your political agency go to waste.

We are on the cusp of just such a political paradigm shift at present and we know how badly that played out in the inter-war years with the rise of fascism throughout the West (not to mention Stalinism in the Soviet Union). It is a situation we should not want to see repeated, especially with the cast of maverick politicians around at present, who are difficult enough to control as it is; figures like Trump, Putin, Lukashenko, Orbán and Bolsonaro immediately come to mind, but others are queuing up behind them equally ill disposed towards dissent (Museveni in Uganda, for example, is following the same playbook, cracking down on opponents both during and after an election contest in an attempt to cling on to power), and equally opposed too, one would imagine, to any changes to the voting system that they have learned to use to their own advantage. This is yet another reason for more campaigning on behalf of proportional representation, which may have its defects but which reduces the scope for that kind of elitist behaviour to prevail. Research into how to create greater proportionality within that system has to remain a priority. Democracy must keep evolving constantly if it is to survive, perhaps even, as I suggested in Chapter 2, to the point of reconsidering the whole issue of presidency and whether it is compatible with democracy at all. It is too easy at present for presidents with extensive executive power to escape accountability by gaming the system. In the worst-case scenarios this can generate presidents for life and that is never a good outcome, no matter what kind of political system we may be talking about.

Dissent v. authoritarianism

Authoritarianism is the natural enemy of dissent and as this study has shown, it can emerge in any social or political context, from the sciences and the arts through to the corporate sector, education and religion. Power of almost any description tends to affect those wielding it that way: they want to extend it and hold on to it as long as they choose, without having to bother about opposition or having to consider the validity of other viewpoints (which they do not believe there can be, belief in their own rightness being apparently limitless). I suspect almost all of us have come up against such a situation at some point in our lives in the workplace, in the person of managers and employers, bullying being one of the insidious methods used to establish such dominance and one that is quite widespread (UK civil servants have increasingly been critical of government ministers over instances of this, for example, and there seems little doubt that it is a recurrent feature of governing circles worldwide). As argued throughout this work, scepticism provides an intellectually highly effective basis for countering this tendency and it should be called into action whenever authoritarianism makes its presence felt, otherwise the latter will seek to dig itself in for the long haul. As we have already noted, authoritarians can always think of reasons for suppressing dissent; almost any kind of crisis can be used to justify this, to the extent of defining it as treasonous to resist the authorities' policies in any manner whatsoever. The situations in Hong Kong and Belarus are topical examples of that response, with the authorities generating the crisis in the first place through their intransigence and then clamping down on protests against it: a cynical, but unfortunately also effective strategy that has a long history of success. Emergency powers can offer almost unlimited scope to the authorities when such situations arise and they need to be monitored scrupulously in every instance to prevent them from getting out of hand in terms of human rights, which they can do only too easily, and frequently. Both the extreme right and the extreme left consider human rights to be an inconvenience to the exercise of their power and will curb them wherever they are allowed to: removing the possibility of openly expressing dissent is the first step towards that goal.

If anything, therefore, dissent is even more needed under an emergency powers regime than in the system in its normal operational mode. Once restricted, civil liberties can be notoriously difficult to win back, especially if it means having to face up to the police or armed forces acting under orders from the regime (who might even resort to martial law to protect themselves, always an available ploy, even in liberal democracies). Dissent, even in its mildest form – public meetings or orderly street marches, for example – can easily be redefined as a breach of the peace, turning the dissenter into a law-breaker and raising the prospect of censorship or even imprisonment (in extreme cases, death). Authoritarian regimes have a long tradition of acting in that way to neutralise opponents and it very often works, boxing dissent into a corner where its options become progressively more limited. When dissent is forced on to the defensive in this manner, then it constitutes a significant victory for the authoritarian temperament in its bid to reshape the political landscape to its own advantage – a bid it will never willingly relinquish, even in the face of concerted civil disobedience (as noted before, the latter often has to turn into violent revolution to bring down such regimes). Perhaps it is only when it is under serious threat from that temperament, as it manifestly is in the contemporary world with its turn to the far right, that we come to recognise the full value of liberal democracy, as well as its inherent precariousness. Democracy may not be dead yet, but it is not very well, with far too much 'displacement of politics' taking place under the aegis of aggressively anti-democratic ideologies.[2]

That precariousness becomes all the more evident when the far right itself is protesting against authoritarianism, a hypocritical stance on its part because it generally wants to replace it with another form of authoritarianism, often more oppressive than the one it is attacking. Free speech can come to mean hate speech, which can come to mean death threats to those opposing it, in a pattern which is becoming all too familiar throughout the Western world (with the US again in the lead). Conspiracy theorists are a classic example of this tendency: dissent that is out to suppress the possibility of dissent against its own position, therefore not true dissent in my reading of it. QAnon is the model here. Right-wing libertarianism also poses a real problem in this respect, appearing to be defending individual freedom against the 'nanny' state, but in reality it is a freedom that benefits only the far right, especially those espousing neoliberal values. Neoliberalism wants no restrictions placed on economic life, which is very much to the advantage of the rich and powerful but hardly to the majority of the working population, who count as nothing better than consumers to the elite trading in the global financial markets. Ever since neoliberalism began to infiltrate Western political life in the last few decades, there has been a growing disparity in wealth between the upper and lower reaches of the economic scale (see economists such as Thomas Piketty on this dispiriting trend[3]), which has put a severe strain on the democratic system. Neoliberalism can often sound close to anarchism, believing that humanity ideally should be subject to no government whatsoever and that regulation of any kind is an evil (taxation featuring high on the hate list, thus the various schemes that exist for the rich to avoid that fate, or at least to keep their contributions to a bare minimum). Basic human rights become hard to guarantee under such a system, where economic power is the prime source of authority. This situation creates considerable difficulties for democracy, especially when the disparities in wealth are rapidly increasing. While I would hope that dissent could come from across the political spectrum, the ideological commitments lying behind it always need to be very carefully scrutinised: authoritarianism is good at disguising itself, as the free speech–hate speech controversy goes on showing us. Seeking to close down opposition can never be an aim of dissent, which is always concerned to open out debate and address issues as publicly as it can, no matter how 'conflicted' the opposed parties may appear to be.[4] Real dissent is not hard to identify.

Dissent and its critical role in society deserve to be taught throughout the school system and on into higher education. Citizenship is not just about being law-abiding, it is also about when it is appropriate, indeed essential if social justice is to be upheld, to object publicly about authorities' incompetence or abuse of power. Education has to be a particularly key area for the dissent project given the threat posed by campaigns such as Turning Point USA and UK, where the notion of law-abiding is perceived in a sinister fashion as outlawing the expression of anything other than far-right-wing views in the classroom. The objective would appear to be to train up a generation of the young to push the system in that direction; a case of building up authoritarianism from ground level by a systematic process of indoctrination, a well-known tactic of fascism in the past (as well as other totalitarian systems like communism or theocracy). The social necessity of dissent, including whistleblowing, ought to be made apparent to all of a society's citizens as well, to make them understand how a democracy cannot function properly without it; and the ability to identify fake dissent will be a further important part of the exercise, given that authoritarians have become so adept at this practice and fall back on it almost by default whenever they are challenged. Manufactured outrage is an authoritarian speciality: Trump's presidency offered a master-class on this and demagogues in general invariably turn to the tactic at the merest hint of criticism. (The shock-jock phenomenon in America has built an empire on it and a highly profitable one too; the late Rush Limbaugh, one of the founders of the genre, was making over $80 million a year by the end of his career, providing his listeners with a steady diet of post-truth.) Increasingly it is a libertarian one too, hence the anti-vaxxer street protests and marches that are becoming so common, with celebrity endorsement playing its part here yet again. The freedom such manufactured outrage purports to be defending is the freedom to make it all but impossible to object publicly to its proponents' ideology, and the freedom to deploy hate speech and death threats to achieve this goal. Fake dissent is not hard to identify either.

Resetting the politics of dissent

This book's concern has been to outline the many ways in which dissent has been put under threat in contemporary society, with politicians, especially of the far right, doing their utmost to remove it from the political process – and unfortunately, it has to be said, succeeding far more than they should have ever been allowed to. The book has also emphasised the critical role that dissent has played, and should still be playing, in our culture as a bulwark against prejudice. Dissent versus authoritarianism is turning into the crucial socio-political issue of our time and we should be under no illusion as to how far the right will be prepared to go in order to win that struggle. Whatever volume of lies and accusations of fake news is required to give it the advantage it seeks it will duly come up with, even to the extent of trying to undermine the faith of the public in their own electoral system, as Trump and his supporters did progressively hysterically in the aftermath of his loss. This was pursued up to the point of inciting mob action to try and prevent Congressional certification of Joe Biden's victory, all on the utterly baseless claim of the election having been stolen. Rejection by the electorate just could not be countenanced by the Trump camp, so it resorted to scare tactics and bullying. This is far-right politics at its most dangerous, suggesting an almost visceral dislike of opposition that bodes ill for the very concept of democracy; in effect, the far right will only be happy with a one-party system – their party, naturally, and their party only, for ever. The politics of dissent therefore urgently needs to be reset to enable it to fulfil its historic role: that is what the dissent project has been designed to achieve. There just has to be far more close scrutiny of authority of every kind across the political spectrum and more protection for whistleblowers, combined with less scope for governments to curtail opposition and dissent from either their parliamentary opponents or the mainstream media.

For starters, elective dictatorship is an area of democratic politics that really ought to have far more checks and balances built into it than currently is the case, hence the earlier survey of what proportional representation in its various forms has to offer. Even if we can never achieve full proportionality, the closer we can get to it the better it will reflect the actual political opinions of the electorate in all their diversity and it can keep being refined to that end: STV, AV, two-ballot and TR do not have to be the end of the line in that respect. The social media scene is also desperately in need of a substantial raft of checks and balances: death threats go well past the boundaries of what can ever be considered to count as acceptable dissent (fake dissent with menace we might call it), as do racism and misogyny. Monitoring the providers and the sites they give room to ought to be a matter of urgency and it is part of dissent's brief to keep lobbying those in power to do that as thoroughly as they can. The surge in usage of social media during the coronavirus pandemic and then the 2020 American presidential election, both of which unleashed an increased volume not just of hate speech but also of conspiracy theories that further intensified already antagonistic partisan divisions, indicates just how dangerous the current set-up in this area is as far as democratic ideals are concerned. The 2020 campaign to persuade major advertisers to withdraw, even if only temporarily, from sites like Facebook which allow hate speech material to be posted (or at the very least are lax in their monitoring of it), is an example of how such lobbying could be made more effective. Admittedly, this was a test case only and had minimal financial impact, but it was a symbolically important one in setting a precedent: a threat to their profit margins is just about the only thing that such entities could not ignore and they have been given a clear warning as to how this could be organised in earnest. That to me qualifies as political agency put to principled use.

Opposition will probably always be seen as an irritant by a ruling group (mere 'carping' as a UK government spokesman recently dismissed it in high-handed fashion[5]), but if it is cowed into submission by those authorities then they will be able to act without restriction, which the historical record suggests is never a good idea if we want to maintain a socially just society. Having to argue a case for this is an indication of just how bad things have become in the liberal democratic world of late, but it is clear that social justice will never survive for long without 'carping' from those outside the ruling elite. This is all the more reason to be critical, sceptical and just plain awkward about what that elite is doing, what it takes for granted – and what it should not be permitted to. The qualification has to be added, however, that carping must not involve evidence made to order in the manner of the conspiracy theorist or far-right extremist. Policy-based evidence-making should never form any part at all of the democratic process, although it has to be noted that the more unscrupulous of our political leaders decided that the pandemic justified them engaging in that activity, largely as a means of covering up their own incompetence. The move from there to claiming that elections are being stolen is not so large a step to take. Demagoguery is not subtle in such matters, nor slow in taking advantage of them.

Racism is an area where the political authorities very definitely need to keep being challenged as publicly and vociferously as possible, given the manifest abuses that it gives rise to internationally that have rarely been addressed with anything like the degree of seriousness they deserve. Black Lives Matter (BLM) has given this issue a much higher profile than it has had for quite some while (depressing though it is that it has taken several deaths to bring this about) and it should not be permitted to lose momentum. This is an example of dissent at its most visible and focused, a cause that the left and centre can give their wholehearted support to as a clear-cut case of official negligence to ensure some of the most basic rights of all citizens within a liberal democratic framework. No-one on the left or centre of the ideological spectrum can be in disagreement with the principles behind such a dissenting initiative, nor on the need to be on guard against any sway towards the racism that is so prevalent in our culture. It is not a matter which needs to be debated as to its pros and cons, it is a case of injustice pure and simple that no human being should ever have to suffer; equal rights have to mean just that and to apply without exception. Protests over racial discrimination put the authorities on the spot and reveal their hypocrisy if they refuse to engage with them to the extent of initiating reform in their public services, as opposed to the more usual practice of empty promises to do so. The police force would be the most obvious target for such an exercise, in the US above all as the spate of incidents since the George Floyd case clearly indicate (from a black perspective America must appear perilously close to being a police state), but it is by no means the only one in need of a radical change of system culture. Bureaucracy in general has a tendency to reflect the prejudices of the government that controls it and an assumption of white superiority is all too often to be found there in the West, simply taken for granted in most cases. The US may be the most glaring example of this at present, but it is by no means the only one that is guilty of such institutionally led discrimination against non-white ethnic groups, regardless of whether they are native-born or not (there is a widespread assumption that your loyalties must lie elsewhere if that is the case). Again, this is a transnational concern that goes beyond the populist nationalisms that have sought to dominate the political landscape in recent years with their racist rhetoric and anti-immigrant campaigns. Dissent will always be on the side of equal rights and always ready to speak up for those being denied them.

Green dissent

The environment provides another source of dissent in terms of the crisis over climate change and the green movement has been at the forefront of this, putting itself into opposition to an entire lifestyle – that of advanced capitalism, with all the economic benefits that entails (in the West at least). Not surprisingly this objective has been very controversial, suggesting to many that it might lead to a much lower standard of living – never a popular idea in a culture as ideologically committed to economic growth as ours, where the public have long been conditioned to expect ever-rising levels of wealth and consumption from generation to generation and can turn against politicians who fail to deliver this without due cause. Yet the Western obsession with economic growth over the last few centuries has culminated in severe, potentially catastrophic, damage to the global environment and although that has now been more or less acknowledged by the majority of national governments (if somewhat reluctantly in most cases), they have still to generate really significant action against the problem, despite the increasingly alarming warnings from various scientific bodies that it may soon be beyond our control to arrest the process. The dreaded tipping points loom ever closer each year – unless you choose to take the QAnon route and regard these as part of yet another conspiracy.

Our systematic abuse of the environment, and the huge increase in carbon emissions it has created, has been a concern of the green movement for some time now and they keep putting the case for a switch to greener energy policies, such as the use of solar, wind and wave power. These alternative sources have been developed up to a certain point (wind farms having the most noticeable effect on the landscape) and when, a few years back, we were thought to be approaching 'peak oil', they gained in public support, looking like the near future of energy production. But the fossil fuel industry has since managed to identify considerable new reserves of oil around the world (they are proving indefatigable on that score) and it is so big and politically powerful that it continues to be the world's major supplier of energy, with little significant check on its activities. National governments in general are reluctant to take on such an adversary, therefore the use of fossil fuel goes on largely unabated, with other energy sources lagging well behind in terms of planning and funding. When governments do try to encourage the development of green energy, it is noticeable that they generally make a point of emphasising its profit potential to prospective investors, as if the environmental benefit was not strong enough on its own. Change in this area has been painfully slow, which suits the vested economic interests only too well; the longer it is delayed, the more of their product they can sell and profits they can rake in. All the more reason for green dissent to be better represented in parliamentary systems and particularly their ruling groups, whereas currently this is fairly intermittent in the West. The UK has only ever had one Green MP, for example, although Green parties have fared somewhat better on the continent than here. That is a situation which constitutes a strong argument for proportional representation, since it opens up the hope of Green politicians coming to have greater involvement in coalition governments and being able to argue their case there. 'First past the post' tends to hamper the chances of emerging political groupings like the Greens, and their cause is far too important for it to be sidelined in that manner. Environmental issues are not mere niche concerns.

The fossil fuel industry offers yet another example of fake dissent in the robust support it has been providing for climate change scepticism, including financing a number of studies that query the scientific data and the conclusions drawn from them. Dissenting on the basis of that body of work means dissenting in the name of profit; in other words, being prejudiced by profit and only accepting conclusions that justify the continuation of the activity that generates it for your company, regardless of the ethics of the policy. It has to be pointed out that climate change scepticism is something of a misnomer in this context and that critics of the industry's position have taken to referring to it as denialism instead. Neither 'dissent' nor 'scepticism' are appropriate terms for such self-serving rejection of overwhelmingly majority scientific opinion, not with its blatantly ulterior motives. It is worrying to note that some politicians have been convinced by denialism, however, with President Trump predictably enough going out of his way to do so, emphatically endorsing the denialists' cause and supporting the fossil fuel industry within America during his term in office. Conspiracy theories abound in this area too and as usual can always find an audience willing to be given a simple answer to a complex problem (and global warming is exceedingly complex in terms of the Earth as a system), with the denialist studies supplying them with just the kind of arguments that they would want in order to construct their notions of 'evidence'. Fake dissent in this case makes it considerably more difficult for international action on climate change to be organised, which is good news to the fossil fuel industry but not to the green movement – or the future generations they are speaking for.

A degrowth movement has also emerged in recent years, arguing that as it is economic growth that is the root of our environmental problems, we should cut back sharply on this (fossil fuel would have to be high on the list for attention). For such theorists as Serge Latouche, it is in fact time to say 'Farewell to Growth' altogether and develop an entirely new socio-political model that radically alters our relationship to the environment in order to stave off disaster.[6] That would be a dissent project on the very largest scale as far as our current way of life is concerned, requiring a complete overhaul of our belief system, and it is a moot point whether it could ever attract enough public support to achieve all of its objectives. It would mean shifting from the present position of regarding the environment as something to be exploited all the way over to regarding it as something to be protected, effectively turning away from the concept of modernity that has underpinned Western culture since the Enlightenment. Nevertheless, it is the kind of dissent that needs to be expressed and that the system ought to be exposed to; if it generates debate about the governmental addiction to growth then that in itself would be useful, given the clearly visible environmental cost of ever-expanding economic growth. As things stand ideologically, growth is simply taken for granted, as if that were the only possible way of running a society (think of how many election campaigns are structured around that topic, even during a pandemic), whereas we ought to be considering its impact on climate change in far more detail and reassessing its role in our culture. The only things that slow growth down to any extent at present are stock market crashes, natural disasters or pandemics, and those can hardly be considered rational solutions for tackling climate change in the longer term. Whenever any of them is brought under control, then growth is promoted again as obsessively as before; for most Western politicians that is just business as usual and they will rarely bother themselves with worrying all that much about its negative impact on the environment.

Green dissent, in both its mainstream and its more radical degrowth sense, should be seen as a necessary component of the dissent project. By challenging accepted wisdom and asking some very pointed questions about Western governmental policy, questions that those governments are highly unlikely to ask themselves, it is not just speaking to, but for, future ages. We ought to reassess economic policy and its environmental impact frequently, and thoroughly, as a standard procedure rather than just assuming that economic growth in itself has to be a good thing; plainly, that is not always the case and green dissent is critical in keeping society acutely aware of just how serious the issues are on this front. It has to be admitted that some green dissent can be extreme, such as that suggesting that degrowth should go to the extent of returning us to a pre-industrial lifestyle with only a fraction of the current global population (a tougher sell in a Western election campaign would be hard to imagine); but the debate that it generates is always going to be really valuable in drawing attention to all the negative effects of a fossil-fuel-based economy, something we cannot be reminded of too much. Green dissent still has much to do, although that has to be considered an indictment of the kind of culture we have developed, where its warnings are still so largely ignored by those in power. This becomes shockingly apparent when we contemplate the wanton destruction ('ecocide' as it is coming to be referred to) of the Amazonian rain forest, yet another casualty of short-term, profit-based, economic thinking. That this was generated by an autocratic 'strong leader', impervious to green arguments (even from within his own nation) and determined to demonstrate to the world just how much power he had to wield, will come as no surprise by now. The sheer machismo of authoritarianism can be a depressing sight to behold and it has been far too much in evidence of late, for all that feminism has done to raise public consciousness about its dangers. Machismo can only distort any political set-up (dictatorship is very much a male phenomenon) and it has to be one of dissent's prime concerns, something to be targeted whenever and wherever it arises in any walk of life. It will always be the enemy of dissent.

Conclusion: democracy and dissent

Returning to the questions posed in the Introduction, it should now be apparent why dissent is necessary, why it is being opposed, who gains from that policy and why, where dissent should be encouraged and implemented, and what we can do individually to aid the cause of dissent. Democracy depends for its success on an oppositional style of politics, where a governing group is constantly being scrutinised and questioned over its policies and their effects by the other parties in a parliamentary setting. Yet unless it goes on from there to include dissent in all its forms – criticism from the mainstream media, whistleblowing, campaigns on issues such as the environment, protest movements such as BLM, Lyotard-style 'little narratives' in general – then it will not be functioning for the full public benefit. There has to be space for both formal and informal opposition, therefore, and dissent in its wider sense operates mainly on that informal side, enlarging the political sphere in democracy in a very positive way. The success of BLM in sparking a global response to racism is a prime example of the critical importance of the informal sector's ability to draw attention to the manifest failings of the authorities over this issue, failings they have consistently not been addressing with anything like the required degree of seriousness or commitment. Add in Extinction Rebellion (XR) and we can see how vitally important informal dissent can be in generating public debate on issues that the authorities would prefer to keep off the political agenda as much as possible, seeking instead to subordinate them to economic matters that are easier to deal with.

Closing off that informal space is a first step on the way to authoritarianism and, ultimately, anti-democratic government – a step that a series of governments internationally have seen fit to take in recent years, offering a template for like-minded authoritarians to access in future. As the coronavirus pandemic revealed, politics can shift into that mode surprisingly easily – and surprisingly quickly too. Almost before you know it, emergency powers can be in place and dissent becomes increasingly difficult to express publicly as sanctions against it are rushed into the statute book. Emergency powers will always hold out an attraction for extremist politicians on both the right and the left, although it is the far right that poses by far the greatest threat on the contemporary political scene, for all its complaints about leftist infiltration into public institutions (as well as claiming the same about BLM and XR). Gaining possession of such powers enables extremists to avoid scrutiny and encourages totalitarian attitudes towards those outside the ruling clique to develop. One-party rule all too frequently follows on from such a situation, at which point Levitsky and Ziblatt's prediction comes true and democracy really does 'die'. One can think of several current world leaders – no prizes for guessing the most obvious contenders (amongst the 2022 variety anyway) – who would not be worried at all by such an outcome, who would in fact welcome it wholeheartedly for the unrestrained exercise of power it would guarantee them. Would-be demagogues are not in short supply on the international political scene; nor are, unfortunately enough, opportunities for them to exert themselves and see how just far they can manage to go in building their own opposition-proof empires. Their answer to being conflicted is to remove those who disagree with them.

A dissent project is not a luxury, therefore, but an absolutely crucial part of the democratic process, without which it will always be at risk from the ambitions of ruthless politicians and their parties. If it appears an irritant to the ruling classes, then that is proof it is doing its job properly. Irritating authority is precisely what dissent ought to be doing, because otherwise authority will take advantage of its power and seek to eradicate pluralism as it centralises power to its own benefit – and that is a situation that can arise in any walk of life. For all the apparent commitment to pluralism in democratic states it is noticeable how keen so many governments are to achieve social homogeneity in their citizens' behaviour and outlook, gradually marginalising all those who think differently in ideological terms: the 'one-dimensional man' that Herbert Marcuse warned us about way back in the 1960s is becoming the goal, with no-one rocking the boat by means of protests or civil disobedience.[7] Both difference and diversity have to struggle to maintain their ideals even in the most democratic of societies. Immigrants tend to be viewed with considerable suspicion almost everywhere in the West these days, for example, and anti-Semitism has been noticeably on the increase, compounding the difficulties that minorities have to contend with. White supremacism is much in evidence overall too, in both explicit and implicit form, and anti-Semitism is an integral part of its DNA. Dissent must keep speaking out against such dangerous developments, otherwise they will become, in Cas Mudde's wording, even more mainstreamed and normalised than they are at present, thus further reinforcing the hold that the far right has over our political life. And just to elaborate on a point made above: the far right can be found operating in any walk of life, not just in politics. Authoritarianism has to be seen as a constant threat, one that is not afraid to break social and political conventions in order to get its way, motivated by an insatiable appetite for power.

We demonstrably need to draw back from our reliance on grand narratives – certainly, uncritical belief in them – which are so often the source of bigotry and prejudice. The twentieth century suffered very badly from these in the forms of communism and fascism, and if the former is now all but gone from the scene, the latter has been making a comeback that is deeply worrying. Fundamentalist religious belief, of any variety, does not help the situation either, raising the spectre of profoundly anti-democratic theocracy: yet another one-dimensional social form that is convinced it is always in the right and that no other world-vision has any validity at all. I would argue that democracy should not be seen as a grand narrative, although some theorists such as Francis Fukuyama do treat liberal democracy in that way and it would be fair to classify the growth-based version of it as such, given its enthusiastic commitment to capitalism.[8] The latter manifestly does qualify as a grand narrative, however, claiming as it does to have all the answers to the world's socio-political and economic problems and to be beyond criticism as a system: a Hegelian-style apex of human development, as it were, which should be kept free from government intervention. Democracy, however, is not a finished product; rather, it is a dynamic entity which can, and definitely should, keep changing as cultures evolve. The electoral system ought to be open to modification to reflect such changes, which could of course include changes to the economic system: as observed before, capitalism (or at least the relatively unfettered style of it that we are lumbered with in the West at present under the guise of neoliberalism) is not an essential element of democracy. As a notable case in point, 'first past the post' is a system long overdue for reassessment, and indeed all electoral systems could do with regular reassessment as to how well they are serving the public – and not just the plainly self-interested party system. Proportional representation, as we have seen, has many forms, but it too is capable of further development in the cause of more accurately capturing the political views of the electorate and increasing the degree of proportionality of every vote cast. Federalism, too, needs to keep being refined to capture the political reality of its constituent parts, as it can be held back by tradition (America gives that impression at present in its reverence for a constitution that is beginning to look seriously outdated in a wide range of respects, providing too many wrong answers to the questions being put to it).

What has to stay a feature, however, no matter what changes do come about, is space for dissent that governments cannot shut down just to make life easier for themselves – and they will undoubtedly keep trying to do that unless vigorously and repeatedly challenged to the contrary. Scope for both formal and informal dissent to be publicly expressed is an essential element to a truly representative democracy; that is, one in which authority is under permanent scrutiny and is not allowed to escape it by attempted abuse of the political system (however disguised). The 2020 American presidential election ought to stand as a particularly sombre warning of how any political system can be abused by those in power and democratic mandates treated with disdain, even in the supposedly liberal West. The worst-case scenario was avoided in this instance, but there is no guarantee that such a situation will not arise again; Trumpism is by no means dead and the next presidential election might well revolve around it, even if Trump himself is not a candidate. What he stands for can still draw on deep support around the nation that can be taken advantage of by some other unscrupulous far-right politician: seventy-four million Americans voted for him in the 2020 election, after all, and a majority really do believe that the election was stolen from them by the Democrats. Add in the storming of the Capitol by an insurrectionary-minded mob and that is a toxic legacy to leave any political system after only one term of office, one that could well take a long time to dissipate too. America has become a test case for Western liberal democracy in the most worrying of ways.

The more dissenting little narratives there are in operation, therefore, in every area of discourse from politics through to religion, science and the arts, then the better it will be for our society: carping is very much in the public interest, as is sowing doubt about the validity of the assumptions that underpin the decisions made by authority. Little narratives are where the politics of dissent can flourish and if the advance of the far right is to be arrested then we will want them to keep asserting themselves, no matter what obstacles may be put in their way by those in power. The authoritarian imperative must not be underestimated; it will turn whatever it can to its own advantage, as the pandemic showed us with the rash of emergency powers that suddenly appeared across the globe, boosting the power of the far right to an alarming, and decidedly undemocratic, degree. It remains to be seen how long it might take to return things to normal in that sphere, to bring back the situation where we are always within opinion (complete with an effective system of check-ups) and debate is both protected and promoted.

That opportunistic reaction alone demonstrates that we need more, not less, dissent in the contemporary world; democracy cannot exist without it. Consider this a heartfelt call to become part of that campaign, to be a contributor to the normalisation and mainstreaming of dissent, which is so vital to guarantee the future of intellectual liberty in our culture, and crucially, to ensure that that dissent is motivated for the correct reasons, to oppose prejudice, bigotry and the lure of conspiracy theory. If democracy is to be kept alive, then we have to ensure that dissent is too. Again, the message to bear firmly in mind when it comes to authority is: be critical, be sceptical, be awkward. Pay no attention to your inner conspiracy theorist and start cultivating your inner dissenter instead.

Notes

1. Butler, 'Critique, Dissent, Disciplinarity', p. 793.
2. See Honig, *Political Theory and the Displacement of Politics*.
3. Piketty, *Capital in the Twenty-First Century*.
4. See Leslie, *Conflicted*.
5. The spokesman was Jacob Rees-Mogg, the leader of the House of Commons, who used the phrase 'endless carping' in a parliamentary debate, to attack both the general public and opposition politicians for complaining about shortages in providing enough Covid-19 tests (see 'Coronavirus: Jacob Rees-Mogg criticises "carping" over tests').
6. See, for example, Latouche, *Farewell to Growth*.
7. For Marcuse, 'containment of social change is perhaps the most singular achievement of advanced industrial society', and one-dimensional man the fairly inevitable outcome of such a process (Marcuse, *One-Dimensional Man*, p. xii).
8. See Fukuyama, *The End of History and the Last Man*.

Bibliography

'About', Turning Point UK, tpointuk.co.uk/about (accessed 6 October 2021).

Adorno, Theodor W., *Negative Dialectics*, trans. E. B. Ashton, London: Routledge & Kegan Paul, [1966] 1973.

Adorno, Theodor W., *Philosophy of Modern Music*, trans. Anne G. Mitchell and Wesley V. Bloomster, London: Sheed & Ward, [1947] 1973.

Agarwal, Pragya, 'Exposing unconscious bias', *New Scientist*, 29 August 2020, pp. 38–42.

Agarwal, Pragya, *Sway: Unravelling Unconscious Bias*, London: Bloomsbury, 2020.

Al-Khalili, Jim, 'Doubt is essential for science – but for politicians it is a sign of weakness', *The Guardian*, 21 April 2020, https://www.theguardian.com/commentisfree/2020/apr/21/doubt-essential-science-politicians-coronavirus (accessed 30 September 2021).

'All that glitters: It is time to do away with flashy science and outlandish claims', *New Scientist*, 22 August 2020, p. 5.

Applebaum, Anne, *Twilight of Democracy: The Failure of Politics and the Parting of Friends*, London: Allen Lane, 2020.

Arendt, Hannah, 'Civil Disobedience', in *Crises of the Republic*, New York: Harcourt Brace Jovanovich, 1972.

Barrow, John D., *Impossibility: The Limits of Science and the Science of Limits*, London: Vintage, 1999.

Barthes, Roland, *Image Music Text*, trans. and ed. Stephen Heath, London: Fontana, 1977.

Baudrillard, Jean, *The Mirror of Production*, trans. Mark Poster, St Louis, MO: Telos Press, [1973] 1975.

Baxter, Richard, *The Saints' Everlasting Rest*, Shallotte, NC: Sovereign Grace, [1650] 2000.

Bayat, Asef, *Life as Politics: How Ordinary People Change the Middle East*, 2nd edn, Stanford, CA: Stanford University Press, 2013.

Beall, Abigail, 'The Milky Way could be home to 5 billion planets like Earth', *New Scientist*, 14 November 2020, p. 14.

Bernstein, Robert L., 'Science and Dissent', *European Review*, 27:1, 2019, pp. 91–6.

Bleiker, Roland, *Popular Dissent, Human Agency and Global Politics*, Cambridge: Cambridge University Press, 2000.

Bloom, Harold, Paul de Man, Jacques Derrida, Geoffrey Hartman and J. Hillis Miller, *Deconstruction and Criticism*, London: Routledge & Kegan Paul, 1979.

Bogdanor, Vernon, *What Is Proportional Representation? A Guide to the Issues*, Oxford: Martin Robertson, 1984.

Bourriaud, Nicolas, 'Altermodern', in Nicolas Bourriaud (ed.), *Altermodern: Tate Triennial*, London: Tate, 2009, pp. 11–24.

Bradley, Doug and Craig Werner, *We Gotta Get Out of This Place: The Soundtrack of the Vietnam War*, Amherst: University of Massachusetts Press, 2015.

Brontë, Charlotte, *Jane Eyre*, ed. Q. D. Leavis, Harmondsworth: Penguin, [1847] 1966.

Brown, Matthew P., 'The Thick Style: Steady Sellers, Textual Aesthetics, and Early Modern Devotional Reading', *PMLA*, 121:1, 2006, pp. 67–86.

Brown, Wendy, *In the Ruins of Neoliberalism: The Rise of Antidemocratic Politics in the West*, New York: Columbia University Press, 2019.

Bunyan, John, *Grace Abounding: With Other Spiritual Autobiographies*, ed. John Stachniewski and Anita Pacheco, Oxford: Oxford University Press, 1998.

Bunyan, John, *Grace Abounding to the Chief of Sinners*, ed. W. R. Owens, Harmondsworth: Penguin, [1666] 1987.

Bunyan, John, *The Pilgrim's Progress*, ed. W. R. Owens, Oxford: Oxford University Press, [1678–84] 2003.

Bunyan, John, 'A Relation of the Imprisonment of Mr John Bunyan', in *Grace Abounding to the Chief of Sinners*, ed. W. R. Owens, Harmondsworth: Penguin, [1666] 1987, pp. 87–110.

Burgess, Michael, *Comparative Federalism: Theory and Practice*, Abingdon and New York: Routledge, 2006.

Burgess, Michael, *Federalism and the European Union: The Building of Europe, 1950–2000*, London: Routledge, 2000.

Busby, Mattha, 'English schools told not to use anti-capitalist material', *The Guardian*, 28 September 2020, p. 13.

Butler, Judith, 'Critique, Dissent, Disciplinarity', *Critical Inquiry*, 35:4, 2009, pp. 773–95.

Caygill, Howard, *On Resistance: A Philosophy of Defiance*, London: Bloomsbury, 2013.

Certeau, Michel de, *The Practice of Everyday Life*, 3rd edn, trans. Steven F. Rendall, Berkeley: University of California Press, [1990] 2011.

Chen, Eddy Keming, 'Welcome to the fuzzy-verse', *New Scientist*, 5 September 2020, pp. 36–40.

Clark, Stuart, 'Measuring up the universe', *New Scientist*, 2 January 2021, pp. 32–8.

Clark, Stuart, 'A quantum twist in space-time', *New Scientist*, 28 November 2020, pp. 34–8.

Collins, Jeffrey R., 'Redeeming the Enlightenment: New Histories of Religious Toleration', *Journal of Modern History*, 81:3, 2009, pp. 607–36.

Collins, Ronald K. L. and David M. Skover, *On Dissent: Its Meaning in America*, New York: Cambridge University Press, 2013.

Collins, Stephen, 'Ireland's voting system: how does it work and how should I use it?', *Irish Times*, 7 February 2020, https://www.irishtimes.com/news/politics/ireland-s-voting-system-how-does-it-work-and-how-should-i-use-it-1.4165178 (accessed 28 September 2021).

'Coronavirus: Jacob Rees-Mogg criticises "carping" over tests', BBC News, 17 September 2020, https://www.bbc.co.uk/news/uk-politics-54194333 (accessed 5 October 2021).

Crane, Leah, 'Why matter exists at all', *New Scientist*, 25 April 2020, p. 14.

Danahar, Paul, *The New Middle East: The World after the Arab Spring*, London: Bloomsbury, 2013.

Deleuze, Gilles and Félix Guattari, *Anti-Oedipus: Capitalism and Schizophrenia*, trans. Robert Hurley, Mark Seem and Helen R. Lane, London: Athlone Press, [1972] 1984.

Deleuze, Gilles and Félix Guattari, *A Thousand Plateaus: Capitalism and Schizophrenia*, trans. Brian Massumi, London: Athlone Press, [1980] 1988.

Dent, Arthur, *The Plaine Mans Path-Way to Heaven*, Amsterdam: Theatrum Orbis Terrarum, [1601] 1974.

Derrida, Jacques, *Resistances of Psychoanalysis*, trans. Peggy Kamuf, Pascale-Anne Brault and Michael Naas, Stanford, CA: Stanford University Press, [1996] 1998.

Derrida, Jacques, *Writing and Difference*, trans. Alan Bass, Chicago: University of Chicago Press, [1967] 1978.

Descartes, René, *Philosophical Writings*, trans. and ed. Elizabeth Anscombe and Peter Thomas Geach, London: Thomas Nelson, 1954.

Diamond, Larry, 'Facing Up to the Democratic Recession', *Journal of Democracy*, 26:1, 2015, pp. 141–55.

Dickens, Charles, *Hard Times: For These Times*, ed. David Craig, Harmondsworth: Penguin, [1854] 1969.

Dorfman, Ben, 'Refractions: Dissent and Memory', in Ben Dorfman (ed.), *Dissent! Refracted: Histories, Aesthetics and Cultures of Dissent*, Frankfurt: Peter Lang, 2016, pp. 11–22.

Eagleton, Terry, *Why Marx Was Right*, 2nd edn, New Haven, CT and London: Yale University Press, [2011] 2018.

'Education Watch', Turning Point UK, tpointuk.co.uk/education-watch (accessed 6 October 2021).

Engels, Friedrich, *Anti-Dühring: Herr Eugen Dühring's Revolution in Science*, Beijing: Foreign Languages Press, [1878] 1976.

Falk, Barbara J., 'The History, Paradoxes, and Utility of Dissent: From State to Global Action', in Ben Dorfman (ed.), *Dissent! Refracted: Histories, Aesthetics and Cultures of Dissent*, Frankfurt: Peter Lang, 2016, pp. 23–50.

Fazackerley, Anna, 'Academics fear naming and shaming for leftwing views', *The Guardian*, 10 March 2020, p. 46.

Frank, Thomas, *One Market under God: Extreme Capitalism, Market Populism and the End of Economic Democracy*, London: Secker & Warburg, 2001.

Frascina, Francis, *Art, Politics and Dissent: Aspects of the Art Left in Sixties America*, Manchester: Manchester University Press, 1999.

Fukuyama, Francis, *The End of History and the Last Man*, London: Hamish Hamilton, 1992.

Gellman, Barton, *Dark Mirror: Edward Snowden and the Surveillance State*, London: Bodley Head, 2020.

Geoghegan, Peter, *Democracy for Sale: Dark Money and Dirty Politics*, London: Head of Zeus, 2020.

Gessen, Masha, *Surviving Autocracy*, London: Granta, 2020.

Ginsburg, Ruth Bader with Mary Hartnett and Wendy W. Williams, *My Own Words*, New York: Simon & Schuster, 2016.

Goldie, Mark, 'The Theory of Religious Intolerance in Restoration England', in Ole Peter Grell, Jonathan I. Israel and Nicholas Tyacke (eds), *From Persecution to Toleration: The Glorious Revolution and Religion in England*, Oxford: Clarendon Press, 1991, pp. 331–68.

Gramsci, Antonio, *Selections from the Prison Notebooks*, trans. and ed. Quintin Hoare and Geoffrey Nowell Smith, London: Lawrence & Wishart, 1971.

Hall, Stuart, *Essential Essays, vol. 1: Foundations of Cultural Studies*, ed. David Morley, Durham, NC: Duke University Press, 2018.

Ham, Ken, *The Lie: Evolution – Genesis – the Key to Defending Your Faith*, Green Forest, AR: Master, 1987.

Harris, Lasana and Daniel Cossins, 'The roots of racism', *New Scientist*, 29 August 2020, pp. 43–5.

Hegel, Georg Wilhelm Friedrich, *The Philosophy of History*, trans. J. Sibree, New York: Dover, [1838] 1956.

Hill, Christopher, *A Turbulent, Seditious, and Factious People: John Bunyan and His Church 1628–1688*, Oxford: Clarendon Press, 1988.

Hilton, Timothy, *Picasso*, London: Thames & Hudson, 1975.

Honig, Bonnie, *Political Theory and the Displacement of Politics*, Ithaca, NY: Cornell University Press, 1993.

Honig, Bonnie, *Public Things: Democracy in Disrepair*, New York: Fordham University Press, 2017.

Honneth, Axel, *The Struggle for Recognition: The Moral Grammar of Social Conflicts*, trans. Joel Anderson, Cambridge: Polity, [1992] 1995.

Hume, David, *Enquiries Concerning Human Understanding and Concerning the Principles of Morals*, ed. L. A. Selby-Bigge, rev. P. H. Nidditch, 3rd edn, Oxford: Clarendon Press, [1748/1751] 1975.

Irigaray, Luce, *An Ethics of Sexual Difference*, trans. Carolyn Burke and Gillian C. Gill, London: Athlone Press, [1984] 1993.

Jencks, Charles, *The Language of Post-Modern Architecture*, 6th edn, London: Academy, 1991.

Joyce, James, *Finnegans Wake*, London: Penguin, [1939] 2000.

Kaminsky, Howard, *A History of the Hussite Revolution*, Eugene, OR: Wipf & Stock, [1967] 2004.

Kant, Immanuel, *Critique of Judgment*, trans. James Creed Meredith, rev. Nicolas Walker, Oxford: Oxford University Press, [1790] 2007.

Kant, Immanuel, *Critique of Practical Reason*, trans. and ed. Mary Gregor, 2nd edn, Cambridge: Cambridge University Press, [1788] 2015.

Kant, Immanuel, *Critique of Pure Reason*, trans. Norman Kemp Smith, London: Macmillan, [1787] 1973.

Kingdon, Robert M. with Thomas A. Lambert, *Reforming Geneva: Discipline, Faith and Anger in Calvin's Geneva*, Geneva: Droz, 2012.

Kleinherenbrink, Arjen, 'New Images of Thought: On Two Kinds of Speculative Realism', *Global Discourse*, 11:1–2, 2021, pp. 83–100.

Kuhn, Thomas S., *The Copernican Revolution: Planetary Astronomy in the Development of Western Thought*, Cambridge, MA: Harvard University Press, 1957.

Kuhn, Thomas S., *The Structure of Scientific Revolutions*, 2nd edn, Chicago and London: University of Chicago Press, 1970.

Laclau, Ernesto and Chantal Mouffe, *Hegemony and Socialist Strategy: Towards a Radical Democratic Politics*, trans. Winston Moore and Paul Cammack, London: Verso, 1985.

Laing, R. D., *The Divided Self: An Existential Study in Sanity and Madness*, London: Penguin, [1960] 2010.

Lakatos, Imre and Alan Musgrave (eds), *Criticism and the Growth of Knowledge*, Cambridge: Cambridge University Press, 1970.

Larson, Heidi J., *Stuck: How Vaccine Rumors Start – And Why They Don't Go Away*, New York: Oxford University Press, 2020.

Latouche, Serge, *Farewell to Growth*, trans. David Macey, Cambridge and Malden, MA: Polity Press, [2007] 2009.

Lawton, Graham, 'The war against reality', *New Scientist*, 19 September 2020, p. 24.

Leslie, Ian, *Conflicted: Why Arguments Are Tearing Us Apart and How They Can Bring Us Together*, London: Faber & Faber, 2021.

Levitsky, Steven and Daniel Ziblatt, *How Democracies Die: What History Reveals about Our Future*, London: Viking, 2018.

Lewis, Barry, 'Postmodernism and Fiction', in Stuart Sim (ed.), *The Routledge Companion to Postmodernism*, 3rd edn, Abingdon and New York: Routledge, 2011, pp. 169–81.

'Life on Venus? We're still looking', *New Scientist*, 19/26 December 2020, pp. 24–5.

Lukács, Georg, *History and Class Consciousness: Studies in Marxist Dialectics*, trans. Rodney Livingstone, 2nd edn, London: Merlin Press, [1922] 1971.

Lyotard, Jean-François, *The Differend: Phrases in Dispute*, trans. Georges Van Den Abbeele, Manchester: Manchester University Press, [1983] 1988.

Lyotard, Jean-François, *Discourse, Figure*, trans. Antony Hudek and Mary Lydon, Minneapolis, MN: University of Minnesota Press, [1971] 2010.

Lyotard, Jean-François, *Heidegger and 'the jews'*, trans. Andreas Michel and Mark S. Roberts, Minneapolis, MN: University of Minnesota Press, [1988] 1990.

Lyotard, Jean-François, *Lessons on the Analytic of the Sublime*, trans. Elizabeth Rottenberg, Stanford, CA: Stanford University Press, [1991] 1994.

Lyotard, Jean-François, *Peregrinations: Law, Form, Event*, New York: Columbia University Press, 1988.

Lyotard, Jean-François, *The Postmodern Condition: A Report on Knowledge*, trans. Geoff Bennington and Brian Massumi, Manchester: Manchester University Press, [1979] 1984.

Lyotard, Jean-François, *The Postmodern Explained to Children: Correspondence 1982–1985*, trans. Don Barry et al., ed. Julian Pefanis and Morgan Thomas, London: Turnaround, [1986] 1992.

Lyotard, Jean-François, 'A Svelte Appendix to the Postmodern Question', in *Political Writings*, trans. Bill Readings and Kevin Paul Geiman, London: UCL Press, 1993.

Lyotard, Jean-François and Jean-Loup Thébaud, *Just Gaming*, trans. Wlad Godzich, Manchester: Manchester University Press, [1979] 1985.

Mandelbrot, Benoit, *The Fractal Geometry of Nature*, New York: W. H. Freeman, 1982.

Mao Tse-tung, *Quotations from Chairman Mao Tse-tung*, Beijing: Foreign Languages Press, 1972.

Marcuse, Herbert, *One-Dimensional Man: Studies in the Ideology of Advanced Industrial Society*, London: Routledge & Kegan Paul, 1964.

Martin, Sean, *The Cathars: The Rise and Fall of the Great Heresy*, Harpenden: Pocket Essentials, [2005] 2014.

Marx, Karl, *Early Writings*, trans. Rodney Livingstone and Gregor Benton, London: Penguin, [1975] 1992.

Marx, Karl and Friedrich Engels, *The Communist Manifesto*, ed. Frederic L. Bender, New York and London: W. W. Norton, [1848] 1988.

Medearis, John, *Why Democracy Is Oppositional*, Cambridge, MA: Harvard University Press, 2015.

Mishra, Pankaj, *Bland Fanatics: Liberals, Race and Empire*, London and New York: Verso, 2020.

Mouffe, Chantal, *For a Left Populism*, London and New York: Verso, 2018.

Mudde, Cas, *The Far Right Today*, Cambridge and Medford, MA: Polity Press, 2019.

Nathan, Aharon, *A Pocket Guide to Total Representation (TR): How to Achieve Simple and Effective Electoral Reform of the Commons and the Lords*, 2nd edn, London: A. Nathan, 2020.

Noueihed, Lin and Alex Warren, *The Battle for the Arab Spring: Revolution, Counter-Revolution and the Making of a New Era*, New Haven, CT and London: Yale University Press, 2012.

Orwell, George, 'The freedom of the press' [1945], *New York Times*, 8 October 1972, https://www.nytimes.com/1972/10/08/archives/the-freedom-of-the-press-orwell.html (accessed 15 July 2020).

Orwell, George, *Nineteen Eighty-Four*, Harmondsworth: Penguin, [1949] 1978.

O'Shea, Stephen, *The Perfect Heresy: The Revolutionary Life and Death of the Medieval Cathars*, London: Profile, 2000.

Piketty, Thomas, *Capital in the Twenty-First Century*, trans. Arthur Goldhammer, Cambridge, MA and London: Belknap Press, [2013] 2014.

Ponting, Clive, *The Right to Know: The Inside Story of the Belgrano Affair*, London: Sphere, 1985.

Priestland, David, *The Red Flag: Communism and the Making of the Modern World*, London: Penguin, 2010.

Professor Watchlist, professorwatchlist.org (accessed 6 October 2021).

Pukelsheim, Friedrich, *Proportional Representation: Apportionment Methods and Their Applications*, 2nd edn, Cham, Switzerland: Springer, 2017.

Radcliffe, Ann, *The Mysteries of Udolpho*, ed. Bonamy Dobrée, Oxford: Oxford University Press, [1794] 1980.

Rancière, Jacques, *Disagreement: Politics and Philosophy*, trans. Julie Rose, Minneapolis, MN: University of Minnesota Press, [1995] 1999.

Rancière, Jacques, *Dissensus: On Politics and Aesthetics*, trans. and ed. Steven Corcoran, London and New York: Continuum, 2010.

Rancière, Jacques, 'The Thinking of Dissensus: Politics and Aesthetics', in Paul Bowman and Richard Stamp (eds), *Reading Rancière: Critical Dissensus*, London and New York: Continuum, 2011, pp. 1–17.

Rex, Richard, *The Lollards*, Basingstoke: Palgrave, 2002.

Riley, Charlotte Lydia (ed.), *The Free Speech Wars: How Did We Get Here and Why Does It Matter?*, Manchester: Manchester University Press, 2020.

Ritchie, Stuart, *Science Fictions: Exposing Fraud, Bias, Negligence and Hype in Science*, London: Bodley Head, 2020.

Rorty, Richard, *Consequences of Pragmatism: Essays 1972–1980*, Brighton: Harvester Press, 1982.

Rovelli, Carlo, *Reality Is Not What It Seems: The Journey to Quantum Gravity*, trans. Simon Carnell and Erica Segre, London: Penguin, [2014] 2017.

Rozell, Mark J. and Clyde Wilcox, *Federalism: A Very Short Introduction*, New York: Oxford University Press, 2019.

Runciman, David, *How Democracy Ends*, London: Profile, 2018.

'Ruth Bader Ginsburg in pictures and her own words', BBC News, 19 September 2020, www.bbc.co.uk/news/world-us-canada-54218139 (accessed 26 September 2020).

Sarat, Austin (ed.), *Dissent in Dangerous Times*, Ann Arbor: University of Michigan Press, 2004.

Schopenhauer, Arthur, *Essays and Aphorisms*, trans. R. J. Hollingdale, Harmondsworth: Penguin, 1970.

Scorer, Richard, 'Save the Children', *New Humanist*, Winter 2020, pp. 22–5.

Seed, John, *Dissenting Histories: Religious Division and the Politics of Memory in Eighteenth-Century England*, Edinburgh: Edinburgh University Press, 2008.

Sim, Stuart, *Lyotard and Politics: A Critical Introduction*, Edinburgh: Edinburgh University Press, 2020.

Sim, Stuart, *Negotiations with Paradox: Narrative Practice and Narrative Form in Bunyan and Defoe*, Hemel Hempstead: Harvester Wheatsheaf, 1990.

Sim, Stuart, *Post-Marxism: An Intellectual History*, London and New York: Routledge, 2000.

Sim, Stuart, *Post-Truth, Scepticism and Power*, Cham, Switzerland: Palgrave Macmillan, 2019.

Sim, Stuart, *Twenty-First Century Puritanism: Why We Need It and How It Can Help Us*, Champaign, IL: Common Ground, 2018.

Smith, David and Julia Carrie Wong, 'QAnon: Trump tacitly backs conspiracy movement', *The Guardian*, 21 August 2020, p. 27.

Smith, Evan, *No Platform: A History of Anti-Fascism, Universities and the Limits of Free Speech*, Abingdon and New York: Routledge, 2020.

'The Stuckist Manifesto', www.stuckism.com/stuckistmanifesto.html (accessed 4 October 2021).

Sunstein, Cass R., *Conspiracy Theories and Other Dangerous Ideas*, New York: Simon & Schuster, 2014.

Sunstein, Cass R., *Why Societies Need Dissent*, Cambridge, MA and London: Harvard University Press, 2003.

Thompson, Frank J., Kenneth K. Wong and Barry G. Rabe, *Trump, the Administrative Presidency, and Federalism*, Washington, DC: Brookings Institution Press, 2020.

Traverso, Enzo, *Left-Wing Melancholia: Marxism, History, and Memory*, New York: Columbia University Press, 2016.

Turning Point USA, tpusa.com (accessed 6 October 2021).

Vasilev, Georgi, *Heresy and the English Reformation: Bogomil-Cathar Influence on Wycliffe, Langland, Tyndale and Milton*, Jefferson: NC: McFarland, 2007.

Wendling, Mike, *Alt-Right: From 4chan to the White House*, London: Pluto Press, 2018.

Wilson, Japhy and Erik Swyngedouw (eds), *The Post-Political and Its Discontents: Spaces of Depoliticisation, Spectres of Radical Politics*, Edinburgh: Edinburgh University Press, 2015.

Zucman, Gabriel, *The Hidden Wealth of Nations: The Scourge of Tax Havens*, trans. Teresa Lavender Fagan, Chicago and London: University of Chicago Press, 2015.

Index